More Kaua'i Tales

More Kaua'i Tales

Frederick B. Wichman

Illustrations by Christine Fayé

Bamboo Ridge Press
Honolulu
1997

ISBN 0-910043-49-3

Published by Bamboo Ridge Press

Designed by Steve Shrader

Printed in the United States

This project has been supported in part by the State Foundation on Culture and the Arts, the Hawai'i Community Foundation, the McInerny Foundation, and the Atherton Family Foundation.

Bamboo Ridge Press is a nonprofit, tax-exempt organization formed to foster the appreciation, understanding, and creation of literary, visual, audio-visual, and performing arts by and about Hawaii's people. Your tax deductible contributions are welcomed.

Bamboo Ridge is supported in part by grants from the State Foundation on Culture and the Arts (SFCA), celebrating over thirty years of culture and the arts in Hawai'i. The SFCA is funded by appropriations from the Hawai'i State Legislature and by grants from the National Endowment for the Arts. Bamboo Ridge Press is a member of the Council of Literary Magazines and Presses.

This is a special issue of *Bamboo Ridge, A Hawai'i Writers Journal,* issue #70
ISSN 0733-0308.

Bamboo Ridge is published twice a year. For subscription information, direct mail orders, or a catalog of our books, call or write:

Bamboo Ridge Press
P.O. Box 61781
Honolulu, Hawai'i 96839-1781
(808) 626-1481

5 4 3 2 1   97 98 99 00 01

Contents

*Dedicated to all those
who have used my stories
in other ways, thus
giving new life to them.
Mahalo.*

Introduction

The events told in these tales occurred at different periods of Kaua'i's history. Living deeds were shaped into narratives, thrilling to hear, edifying in their moralities, and instructive in lessons of good manners and proper behavior. Like all good stories, they were and are designed to entertain as well as keep alive the history and ancestors of the listeners.

The first known settlers of Kaua'i arrived around 300 A.D. and settled along the banks of the Waimea River. For a short time, canoes sailed back and forth into the South Seas bringing new settlers including the Menehune, who were curious explorers. Maliu found the freshwater spring bubbling up on the reef at Moloa'a as the Menehune slowly circled their new homeland.

They were also master builders who solved complicated engineering problems and worked to strict rules of conduct as illustrated in the story of 'Alekoko, the fishpond of Niumalu.

Perhaps during this time a canoe reached the shores of South America and brought back the first sweet potato plants. Certainly the story of Kakala and 'A'awa, two Mū transformed into voracious caterpillars, indicates an early knowledge of that plant and its association with the Mū, a wild and primitive people who also arrived during the earliest period.

The first settlers brought their histories and place names with them. The ancient names and stories were firmly anchored to the new land. On Kaua'i, Hiku lived at the top of Pōki'i Ridge on the edge of the deep canyon at Pu'ukāpele where hardwood trees were farmed to make canoes and weapons and Kawelu lived at the foot of Pōki'i Ridge, a land of heat, marshes, and lakes near the undersea land of the dead.

About 1100 A.D., a group from the Marquesas Islands settled along the banks of the Wailua River. Soon the god Lono arrived with travelers from Rai'atea. The story of Māmā-akua-Lono illustrates the worship of Lono as a private, individual ceremony offered in deep faith.

There were also travelers from Tahiti and other southern islands. The story of Ka Moena Hohola o Mānā illustrates the deep love for one's new home as well as reminds the listener that no other island has such beaches.

For a century and a half, more or less from 1200 to 1350 A.D., the Waimea and Wailua kingdoms fought each other for control of the entire island. It was a time of great heroes and brave deeds which ended when Kūkona of Wailua finally unified Kaua'i. During his time, three sisters arrived in separate canoes. One, Kapo-'ula-kīna'u, toured the island seeking husbands for her bevy of women. One incident of her stay is recounted in Hanakā'ape, the first time she took possession of another's body and spirit in Hawai'i.

The second sister to arrive was Pele. She fell in love with chief Lohi'au of Hā'ena. Because of this love, Pele often returns, even to this day, and revenges herself on anyone brash enough to insult her with bad manners. The tale of Weoweo-pilau is one example of Pele's retribution.

Between 1350 and 1700 A.D., Kaua'i lived in peace. No wars were fought on the island. Therefore, many local heroes had to go to other islands to win their fame after a childhood spent in the nurturing spiritual power for which Kaua'i was famous. One such hero was Pīkoi, and the story of how he won his immense skills is told in the tale of Pīkoi and Puapualenalena.

During these peaceful years, population increased, food supplies kept pace, and storytellers flourished. Naturally, certain farmers were greedy and unkind, two sins in the Kaua'i moral code. So tales like that of 'Ualaka'a came into being, a code of ethics embedded within laughter.

The storytellers created stories of plants unique to Kaua'i such as the 'ōhelo, a member of the cranberry family, one of the very few edible endemic plants. The plant was personified so that its uniqueness was fixed in the memory.

The choosing of a lifelong mate was not always easy. The story of Mali'o, one of many wife-wooing tales, embodies many facets of chiefly life: marriage is a duty to the people; the choice of mates should be mutual; wooing is not a simple affair but often quite complicated; the words of an elder are often the key to success. Sometimes seemingly supernatural help was needed as Mali'o learned when he wooed Ua. Although Mali'o and Ua are gone and no one lives in the valley of Koai'e, the waterfall still tumbles into the pond.

Ordinary events were also turned into stories, such as the tale of Kahalahala. Here the peacefulness of daily social life was shattered by a breach, and such a transgression had to be immediately suppressed, and its story told as a warning to others.

Mermaids were to be seen here and there; they all had long hair and always sat on a favorite rock to comb their tresses. Palai, one such maiden, lived within the lower wet cave of Hā'ena and when the last sight of her hair floating on the water disappeared under the onslaught of modern trash, there were those who mourned the passing of an older, better regulated time.

There was time for laughter, too. Birdcatchers stayed in the mountains for months at a time collecting the feathers of the brilliantly colored honeycreepers. A pair of brothers caught the imagination, and many stories were told about them.

Those who stroll through the high forests know that 'Elepaio's curiosity is still as strong as it ever was.

Tales of the Birdcatcher Brothers were immensely popular. Wa'awa'a-iki-na'au-ao means "a clever but slightly imbecilic person." Wa'awa'a-iki-na'au-pō means "a dumb imbecile." Their stories illustrate the foibles of human action as a source of merriment.

In 1824, the ancient and separate kingdom of Kaua'i ended in a bloody battle which pitted one army with traditional wooden weapons against an invader armed with rifles, bayonets and howitzers. Almost the entire chiefly class of Kaua'i died in that one battle and during the two weeks of deliberate killing that followed. The invader had won, but the story of Pāmāhoa remains as a lamentation for all that has been lost.

When the Menehune had finished building the great irrigation ditch of Kīkī-a-Ola in Waimea Valley and the long fishpond wall of ʻAlekoko, they began to explore this island of Kauaʻi. The band, led by the luna Poʻonui, moved slowly along the coast of Koʻolau and after some time found a cliff ledge ideal for their jumping-into-the-ocean sport at Moloaʻa.

ʻIomo was the favorite game of the Menehune. A player threw a small pebble into the ocean from the edge of a precipice and leapt after it, feet first, entering the water without causing a splash. Then the player had to find and grab the rock before it could sink into the darkness and settle on the ocean floor.

To a people who enjoyed gambling, ʻiomo was ideal. One could bet on how many rocks he or she could recover during the night of playing. Another would bet on his or her ability to enter the ocean splashless. A third would bet on the abilities of a friend. There were many bets offered and taken, and, because the Menehune were a cheerful people, many jokes were told. This one had red eyes from taking so long underwater to find his stone; that one remained clear-eyed but a constant loser for he could never find his stone because he was afraid to open his eyes underwater.

The cape at Ka-lae-o-ʻulu-ʻoma was ideal. A reasonably high cliff had open water at its foot. Beside it was a reef where the jumper could easily climb back onto shore, hike up the trail, and so be back at his jumping off place, ready to take his turn again. These Menehune had nothing else to do. The Menehune slept during the day and played or worked only at night. They did not have to search for food, for the reef was full of fish, octopus, and lipoa seaweed. It was not necessary for them to communicate with the Hawaiian families that lived in Moloaʻa Valley, for the Hawaiians worked during the day and slept at night. Their only chore was to climb into the mountains to fetch cool, fresh, sweet water for them to drink. The Menehune did not like the warm, somewhat brackish water along the shores, but outside of this, these Menehune were completely content.

All except Maliu. He was young, short, and somewhat bow-legged; his beard was not yet fully grown, and he had asthma. There were times when he could not catch his breath. So he learned to go slowly and look carefully at everything around him. His curiosity was great so that each step brought new questions. But no one could answer his questions, and so he learned to observe and memorize and figure out the whys and wherefores for himself.

There were times when the chills caused by the night winds blowing over his wet body brought on the asthma, and he had to fight hard for enough air to breathe. But he leapt like the rest of them, and all his companions knew he had asthma so they did not tease him because he could not run up the hill as fast as they or jump into the ocean as often each night. Everyone expected Maliu to be slow or struggling for breath and never questioned that they did not often see him at the top of Ulu'oma cliff.

As the nights passed, Maliu came to Ulu'oma less and less, for he had found something much more to his liking to do. One evening, as he stopped to look at the view and catch his breath, the sound of laughter flowed down the ridge. Curious, Maliu followed the sound. He passed the hill of Pu'uweuweu where ocean-going birds nested after their long day's journey. He came upon a hālau, a long shed with a thatched roof and walls of woven lauhala. He stood at the door to watch because he had never seen so many strangers together in one place at one time and he was very curious.

Around the wall stood many people, chatting, laughing, hooting, and calling to the five women and five men seated facing each other across a long length of kapa. The kapa would be thrown over the one group of five, and there would be rustling and giggles. Then at the call "Pūhenehene," the group was uncovered. Then the five who had not been covered whispered to one another and looked keenly across to the other five. Then, at last, one of the five would take up a wand decorated with a tuft of feathers and point to one of the other five. Then there would be much laughter, for, Maliu discovered, the object of the game was for one team to hide a small pebble somewhere on the five bodies or in their clothes while the other team guessed where the pebble was.

This seemed to Maliu a much more sensible use for stones on a chilly night. He was about to return to Ulu'oma when one of the men angrily rose from his place and brushed past Maliu to disappear into the night. One of the women looked up at Maliu with a mischievous smile and said, "Won't the stranger take the empty place?"

The other players urged him to join the game. Strangers were always welcome for the news they brought, and a Menehune would have much to tell them of the wonders of which they had heard rumors.

So, for the first time, Maliu played the game of pūhenehene. He was not, for the first few nights, very good at it, for his attention was always on the woman who had smiled at him. When she invited him to walk with her in the moonlight to her house and then invited him inside to sit comfortably on the hikieʻe and then pulled the kapa blanket up over them to keep them warm, Maliu was lost in her smile. From that night on, his name for her was Minoʻaka, Laughing Dimple.

From time to time, Maliu would return to Uluʻoma to join his companions playing ʻiomo. But he much preferred the game of pūhenehene in the hills above Puʻuweuweu.

Many months later the woman with the wondrous smile presented Maliu with a child. More enchanted than ever, Maliu stayed with his wife and child and forgot all about ʻiomo and his companions at Uluʻoma.

One night the Menehune chief Poʻonui began to take mental note of his men as they passed him. One face never passed in front of Poʻonui, and, at last, he called all the Menehune around him and asked: "Where is Maliu?"

The Menehune looked blank.

"When did you see him last?" Poʻonui asked.

There was much discussion. One man claimed to have seen him five minutes ago; another that he'd seen Maliu last night. In the end, everyone agreed no one had seen Maliu for many nights indeed.

"Go, and find him," Poʻonui ordered. "Go, and turn over every rock and leaf, look in every cave and along the reef, but find him."

The Menehune gave so loud a shout that the birds at Puʻuweuweu woke up and flew about in great confusion.

Maliu and Minoʻaka also heard the shout.

"What is that?" she asked.

"My people," Maliu replied sadly. "They have finally realized I have not been with them. Poʻonui probably suspects I am living with you Hawaiians."

"And are you not happy?" she asked, with that smile that had been his downfall.

"Of course," Maliu replied, "but it is against the Menehune law for a Menehune man to live with a Hawaiian woman."

"What will happen to you if they do find you?" she asked.

"I shall die the makepaʻu, the death by being turned into stone," he said sadly. He had seen his friend Pākamoi turned into a rock for stealing a melon from a farmer.

She shuddered. "You must persuade your chief to let you live," she said.

"What gift could I possibly give him?" he asked.

"The gift of cool fresh water at the seaside," Minoʻaka replied.

"Easily said, impossible to do," Maliu said.

"There is a broad, long rock on the reef. Beside it is a hole, now covered with sand," Minoʻaka said, and said no more, for she knew Maliu was clever and would not miss her meaning.

"Yes, I know that rock," he replied, his mind racing.

"You will think of a way to avoid makepaʻu. How could I explain to our child that his father is a rock?" And she turned to the baby and tickled it and cooed over it so that he would remember her smile and not her tears. She realized that if Maliu could persuade Poʻonui not to kill him, the price would be never to see his wife and child again. It was not a pleasant choice, but maybe, if he lived, he could come back from time to time.

Maliu rose from his bed, embraced his wife and child for perhaps the very last time, and slipped out of the house Moving from tree to tree, bush to bush, clump of grass to clump of grass, Maliu went unnoticed down to the reef below the cape of Uluʻoma to a broad, flat rock in the middle of the reef.

When Maliu heard the first shouts that announced he was discovered, he quickly turned, sat down on this broad, flat rock and began to root and wallow like a pig in the ocean to one side of the rock.

When Poʻonui arrived, he demanded, "What are you doing?"

Maliu said, "I am trying to dig down in this place. If I can dig deep enough, cool fresh water like the mountain water you love will come gushing up. Once you taste it, you will know the truth of my words. So I am just digging down to find this delicious water."

"You will not find fresh water on a reef," Poʻonui said.

"Are you so sure?" Maliu asked. "Let my friends help me, and we will find it all the more quickly."

"You are a fool," Po'onui said warmly. "I will order men to dig, but if we do not find fresh water, you will be turned into a stone on the spot."

In no time at all, the Menehune indeed found a spring of fresh water gushing up through the salt water. Here the wai, fresh water, did not mingle with the kai, salt water, and remained cool and sweet. No one had ever heard of such a thing.

Po'onui stood on one end of the long, broad, flat rock, and Maliu stood at the other end. Maliu said to his chief. "He wai hu'ihu'i keia, he wai mānalo, this is the spring of mountain cool water, drinkable water." Maliu held out a coconut cup filled with water.

Po'onui sipped from the cup while he considered Maliu's words. On one level, the words were straightforward and clear. On another, hidden level, what was the meaning? Po'onui was sure that somehow or another Maliu had broken a Menehune law and deserved to be turned into stone. Yet he had found a spring of fresh water where no one had ever thought to find such a thing. He had referred to the water as hu'ihu'i, which means cold as mountain spring water is cold, but also meaning the numbness that is caused by such coldness or by the heat of love. Maliu had also said the water was mānalo, potable or drinkable, which also means to mollify anger, or to be safe from harm or danger. Double meanings, for to the Menehune no words were without hidden meanings. Was the message, "I am in love, let your anger be cooled by this water"?

Then Po'onui laughed. "You shall not die," he said. "Such good work as you have done only brings good fortune, for now we have fresh water to drink."

At the same time Po'onui knew it was time to leave Moloa'a.

Maliu lived, but he never saw his wife or child again.

Maliu's child grew up in the midst of his large Hawaiian family, a hapa Menehune of the ancient time, whose children remained behind when all the Menehune left Kaua'i forever.

The Menehune gave a name to the spring that came bubbling up from under the special broad, flat rock at the foot of Ka-lae-o-'ulu-'oma. They called it Ka-wai-o-Maliu, The-spring-dug-by-Maliu. This spring became a very famous place on the Moloa'a beach from that time forward and may still be bubbling there today.

The sun shone day after day after day. No clouds formed in the sky, no mists hung over the edges of the cliffs from Kawaikini to Maunahina. Without the clouds, no rain fell. Without the rain, the river which they called Wainiha, the angry rushing stream, began to dry up. ʻAʻawa and her husband Kakala themselves never remembered such a period of drought; no one living in their village in the remote end of the valley could remember such a dryness.

For a time, there was no concern. ʻAʻawa and Kakala could find food as they always had, for maiʻa, bananas, grew everywhere from the river's edge far up the steep cliffs, anywhere a farmer could reach and plant. ʻAʻawa and Kakala were Mū, a short people who had found their way to the island of Kauaʻi a long, long time ago. When the red-sailed canoes had come with a strange people from Kahiki who settled the lowlands, the Mū retired into the deep valleys where, in any case, the banana grew. They kept apart from the strangers. They needed none of the plants the new settlers had brought with them, for to the Mū, the banana was everything.

Banana leaves, woven and dried, were the walls and roofs of their houses. Banana leaves, freshly picked, were all the clothes they needed. Banana stump, well rotted, healed the cuts and broken bones they sustained as they farmed the steep cliffs of Wainiha. The fruit was their food, large bunches hanging from the highest rafter of their houses were all they needed. There were also ʻōpae, fresh water shrimp, and wī, delicious snails that hid under the rocks in the river, hōʻiʻo, fiddleheads of fern, and ʻōʻopu, goby fish caught in bamboo traps, welcome additions to their steady diet of banana. This one plant was enough.

Days passed, each as dry as the one before. One moon bloomed in the sky, then faded. Another moon came and the days in between remained without rain. The water of the Wainiha slowed and the ʻōʻopu and wī and ʻōpae deserted their rocks and pools.

Kakala and ʻAʻawa tended their banana plants as best they could. They formed cups from banana leaves and carried water to their newly planted trees.

Kakala smiled at his wife. "Soon it will rain again," he said.

'A'awa nodded. She did not glance into the sky. The dryness of her skin told her more than she wanted to know.

But it did not rain. The sun shone on the plants that were now turning brown. The bananas began to wilt and their trunks, needing water to sustain themselves erect, bent and the plants began to fall. 'A'awa and Kakala gathered whatever bunches of fruit that had matured enough and hung them in their house.

The day came when there were no banana plants left standing with any fruit on them. The chief of the Mū called his people together.

"The trees are dying," he said, "and we will die with them if we stay here."

"Where can we go?" asked one.

"Down to the lowlands," replied another. "Where else can we go?"

"They still have food," said a third.

"Maybe not," said the first. "I have not seen any of their fires at night for a while now."

"They will have gone someplace," said the second. "We must find them."

"We are agreed to go?" asked the chief.

"Yes," said the people. It was frightening to leave their home, even more frightening to go down amongst the newcomers, but food was scarce now and if the rain did not come, there would soon be nothing to eat.

"No," said Kakala.

"We will not go," said 'A'awa. "This is home. The rains will come."

"You are wrong," the chief said. "The rains will never come again and even if they did, it would take months for a banana tree to grow from a huli to the fruit. What will you eat in the meantime?"

"We will find something," 'A'awa said. "I do not wish to go among those people down there." She gestured to the lowlands. "The few times we have met them, they have called us names and thrown things at us. They are not friendly. I do not wish to live among them."

"As you wish," the chief replied. "Stay here. May our god Lono smile upon you and bring you long life."

The next day, Kakala and 'A'awa were alone in the narrow-sided valley. Their neighbors were gone. The sun continued to shine and rain did not come.

They prayed to their god:

> *O, Lono of the low growing banana, mai'a ha'a,*
> *Of the tall, wild banana, mai'a 'a'ao,*
> *Of the black-stemmed banana, mai'a 'ele'ele*
> *Of the seeded banana, mai'a 'ano'ano,*
> *Of the yellow-stemmed banana, mai'a 'au lena,*
> *Send the rain that we may live.*

Still the rain did not come. The river dried up completely. Kakala would try to save his food so that 'A'awa would have enough to eat. She refused to eat unless he swallowed his share of the little they found. They both grew gaunt and the flesh melted from their bones and their teeth loosened. Now they could no longer search among the river rocks for a pool of water they could give to their mai'a. They were now too weak.

Then, one day as they sat under the shade of a lehua tree while the sun blazed down, Kakala said, "We must seek food down below."

'A'awa said, "I know." She looked at her husband. He was nothing but a walking skeleton. She was afraid for him. "We will go this evening when it is cool. The moon will be bright and we can find our way."

"And no one will see us," teased Kakala, for he knew his wife did not like the malihini, the newcomers to their land, looking at her.

She smiled faintly. "They will not like what they will see," she replied. "Two sets of bones walking down the path." She patted his hand. "We will go tonight. Let us sleep and get some rest."

Kakala leaned his head back against the trunk of the tree and closed his eyes. 'A'awa looked at him as he slept. They had been together for many years. She had chosen him from the young men of their people. They had never had children and so they clung closer and closer to one another for they were the only ones in their lives, these two, Kakala and 'A'awa. They did everything together. In time they had come to think so much alike that one could speak for the other without error. He was her life and she was deeply worried. She wondered, as he slept, if they had waited too long before following the others.

That night, they left their home and walked down the narrow path beside the silent river. They walked slowly for they were weak with hunger.

"What would you like to eat?" 'A'awa said.

"A banana," Kakala replied. "Any kind of a banana. And you?"

"Like you, any banana will do," 'A'awa said, "any banana at all. But I must admit I am curious as to what kind of food these malihini eat."

"I must rest," Kakala said. He sat down on the trail and leaned against a rock. "I must rest for a little while."

"Of course. We have plenty of time. Tomorrow morning we shall eat again," 'A'awa said, sitting beside him. Again she wondered if they had waited too long to leave. She prayed to Lono:

> *Lono, god of the Mū,*
> *God of the banana-eating people,*
> *Hear my prayer.*
> *Let my husband live.*

By dawn they had reached the shore where the river used to flow out to sea. The land was silent. The sun shone, the sky was blue, no wind stirred the leaves, no voices broke the silence, just the steady murmur of the sea on the shore. The land here was even drier than it had been up the valley. The people had left.

"You must follow them," Kakala said.

"You? Not I alone. We two together shall go," 'A'awa said strongly.

They rested during the worst of the day and then climbed the hill and looked down into Lumahai Valley. But here too the river was dry and the ground was parched and the people had left. The two clung to each other and trudged along the beach, over Kahalahala Hill, and down onto the land of the great crescent bay stretching from Makahoa Point to Pu'upōā Point.

At Wai'oli they came upon a family of malihini still remaining there. The malihini woman took one look at them and waved them away.

"Give us something to eat," pleaded Kakala.

"Go away," the woman shouted. "There is plenty of food in the sea. Help yourself."

"We do not know how to fish," said Kakala. "I do not know how to use a canoe, even if we had one. Besides, I am too weak."

"That has nothing to do with me," said the woman. "Go away. There is no food here for you."

'A'awa and Kakala continued on. What else could they do? Kakala faltered and would have fallen if 'A'awa had not caught him and helped him ease down to the ground. "I am tired," he said.

"Rest," 'A'awa said. "Rest."

"Soon it will be the long rest," Kakala said. "I am very tired."

"We will soon find food," 'A'awa said. "Do not give up now. Tomorrow we will find some food. Now sleep."

As her husband slept, 'A'awa felt the stirring of anger deep inside her. The malihini woman had been rude. There had been food of some sort, 'A'awa was sure. Some food, or she would not have looked so plump. She and Kakala would have paid back their debt of food some-how or other once they had regained their strength and health. Did the woman have to be so stingy? So uncaring?

Kakala's breath faltered and 'A'awa's stomach leaped into her throat.

> *O, Lono, god of the Mū people,*
> *Let my husband live!*
> *Take me instead.*

Then Kakala's eyes opened and he smiled. "We must continue on," he said. The two of them struggled on, growing weaker and weaker as they went.

They could never have told how many days they walked. One foot went in front of the other and the distance was crossed. 'A'awa did not know what kept Kakala going but she knew that only her rage kept her on her feet. She could recall every detail of the malihini woman, every motion of her hands as she waved them away, refusing their plea for food. Some day, 'A'awa swore to Lono, she would repay that injury.

At last they came to the top of a hill and looked down upon a valley so much smaller than Wainiha, but around the houses there were fields filled with vines such as they had never seen before. They could see men and women going and coming from a spring of water that still miraculously flowed, where they filled calabashes and watered each vine whose leaves were green and flourishing. As the sunset flared in the sky behind them, ʻAʻawa and Kakala watched the people dig under a vine and uncover large tubers. These were carried back to the village and soon the two starving Mū smelled something delicious broiling over a fire.The aroma was strong; it spoke of life and a full stomach. Kakala and ʻAʻawa rose as quickly as they could and struggled down the hill.

They were met at the edge of the fields by two malihini men. "What do you want here?" they demanded, clenching their fists.

"We seek food," Kakala said.

"There is no food here," the men replied "Be off with you."

"There is no food," said Kakala as though he was dreaming. "There is no food and this is the end of the journey." He sank slowly to his knees.

"There is food," ʻAʻawa said. "I can smell it. So can you. Feed us, and we shall become your slaves."

"We have no need of slaves," the men replied. "Go away. There is no food for you here."

"I ask for my husband, not myself. Give him something to eat," pleaded ʻAʻawa.

"No," replied the men. "Not for him, not for you. If we fed everyone who came begging, we would have nothing for ourselves. Go away."

"There is food, I've heard, in that direction," said one man, pointing to the south.

"Go!" said the other man, raising his ʻoʻo, his digging stick of red kauila wood, and threatening to jab them.

ʻAʻawa laughed angrily. "What will you do? Kill us? Your way would be kinder and quicker. No, we will not leave here. Indeed, we have no strength left to go anywhere." She sank to the ground beside Kakala.

With many backward glances, the men left them there on the edge of the green field of green vines. ʻAʻawa cradled Kakala's head on her lap. From time to time, during the rest of that day, they talked of their past life, of the pleasures they had shared, congratulating themselves that they had no children to suffer as they were now. A lifetime was relived in a few hours.

As the sun sank, Kakala sighed and breathed no more. ʻAʻawa held him in her arms and she felt a rage so strong she wondered how her body could possibly contain it. Her rage grew and consumed her and absorbed the body of Kakala and changed them both. During the night, ʻAʻawa and Kakala disappeared. In their place, crawling into the edges of the fields of vines, were two caterpillars, ke kakala and ke ʻaʻawa.

"Eat," whispered the voice of Lono, the god of the Mū. "Eat as much of these ʻuala, the sweet potato, as you can. I set a test for these malihini. I gave them an island of water and rain and fertile soil and brought them a new plant to grow for food. But their hearts are selfish. They do not know that any hospitality given by them will return to them someday when they need it. Let them learn from you, ʻaʻawa and kakala. Eat the sweet potato leaves. If you eat enough, the ʻuala will not grow and these malihini will know what it is to be hungry. Eat!" whispered Lono.

To this day, the caterpillars, the kakala and the ʻaʻawa, eat the leaves of the sweet potato vines. They are hard to see, little green things against green leaves. They are very hungry and obey the command of Lono: "Eat!"

'Alekoko

CHRISTINE FAYE 97©

wo chiefs, a brother and sister, finding that the settlement at Waimea was getting too crowded, moved their people to the banks of a large river that flowed into a distant bay. The brother settled on the north side of this river while the sister built a village on the other side.

The hillsides protecting these settlements were covered with forests of wiliwili, kou, and milo trees that protected the village from heavy winds. Huge waves that dashed against the outer shores were gentled by arms of land as they entered the bay. It was a peaceful and fruitful place to live, and the people were content. They named this bay after the trees, Nāwiliwili.

Brother and sister constantly competed with each other. They loved nalu he'e, the sport of riding the surf on boards, and day after day they bet on who could ride a wave farther and longer than the other. So often were they in the ocean that the people began to call the brother Manō, because he cut through the water as swiftly as a shark, and the sister Hāhālua, for she swam with the dignity and ease of the great manta rays that often came into the bay.

Even though they competed against each other, these chiefs ruled their people well and often met to discuss their mutual problems. At one of these meetings, Manō said, "We do not have a good constant source of fish."

Hāhālua replied, "Of course we have fish. The bay is full of fish. I can catch more fish than you any day."

Manō ignored her taunt. "Be serious. You know there is not good fishing every day of the year. Sometimes we run out of dried fish when the storms come and the seas run high. Then our canoes cannot get out of the bay."

"You're right." said Hāhālua. "And I don't like dried fish. But what can we do about it?"

"Listen," said Manō. "You know how our river meanders along the flat lands below the waterfall. It loops from side to side. What would happen if we built a wall across one of those loops?"

"I see," Hāhālua said. Indeed, in her mind she saw such a loop near her village. Put a wall across that and inside there would be a pond where fish could be farmed. Already certain farmers were raising fish in their taro patches. It would not be impossible to do. "And I know exactly where to build it," Hāhālua said.

"Do you?" the brother asked. "I wonder if we are thinking about the same place."

" I can grow more fish than you, and I'll prove it," Hāhālua said.

"It's a bet," Manō said.

Hāhālua stared at the river for a time. Then she said to her brother, "We will have to move a lot of dirt and gather many rocks. We will have to learn how to keep such a wall from being broken by the river when it is flooding. But I don't see how our people can do such a thing. There are too few of us, and we are still busy digging the irrigation ditches we need for our taro fields."

"True, very true," replied Manō. "But haven't you heard what our cousin Ola of Waimea has done? He asked the Menehune to build him an irrigation ditch around the cliff of Paliuli. Why couldn't the Menehune build our fishponds?"

Hāhālua said, "We can ask them if they will do this for us."

They sent a priest with their request to find the chief of the Menehune, and in a few days the priest returned with a small bearded man walking beside him. The chiefs immediately recognized him as a Menehune and quickly ordered a feast prepared for his welcome.

During the afternoon, the Menehune and the two chiefs walked up one side of the river and down the other side. Then the Menehune borrowed a canoe and sailed up and down the river, often going ashore, and always with the air of someone who looked at a thing once and never forgot it.

Then the small man joined the brother and sister in the shade of a wiliwili tree on the brow of the hill overlooking the river. The Menehune said, "My name is Papa'ena'ena, and I am the chief of the Menehune people. Tell me exactly what you want done."

Hāhālua said, "On the south shore near my village, I'd like a wall built across one loop of the river so that we can have a fishpond."

Manō said, pointing, "On the north side just there, I also want a fishpond, a large one that will hold thousands of pālāmoi, the young fish that we can raise until they become the delicious large threadfin fish, the moi."

"I know where you want your fishpond," the Menehune said to Hāhālua. "It can be done."
Hāhālua smiled with great satisfaction.

Papaʻenaʻena turned to the brother. "I know where you want your fishpond, and I say to you, the loop is too big. Choose another place."

Manō shook his head. "Big, indeed, but it would be used to feed my people for centuries to come. Besides, there is no other place on my side of the river."

Hāhālua's smile grew brighter. She had not forgotten their bet.

The Menehune said, "You are right. There is no other place. For Hāhālua's dam we can bring the rocks from the beach of Makaliʻi, which is nearby. But for the long dam, we will have to bring stones from the plains of Wahiawa."

The Menehune fell silent, planning what needed to be done.

Hāhālua asked, "You say these fishpond dams can be built. But we have not yet talked about what we can do to repay you for such efforts."

"It is good that you have asked that," the Menehune said. "Our price is this. You will allow us to eat of the fish grown in your ponds. For every fish you eat, you will put one aside for the Menehune."

"It is agreed," replied both brother and sister.

"In addition," the Menehune warned, "there are conditions you must follow during the construction of these fishponds. You know we Menehune will work only one night on any project. If we cannot finish it in that time, we will never return to it. We must not be disturbed. You and all your people must remain inside for that night, from the setting of the sun over Hāʻupu Mountain above us to the rising of the sun from the east. Roosters must not crow. All dogs and pigs must be kept from making any noise at all. No one, no one at all must spy on us as we work, for if they do we will leave."

The brother and sister agreed. "We will see these conditions are met," they said, for they were eager to have their fishponds.

"Then get yourselves ready. At the next full moon we will do our work. Remember my conditions."

Papaʻenaʻena left them and returned to his home in the mountains.

Brother and sister called their people together and told them the good news and told them of the conditions set by the Menehune. "Be ready," they warned. "Do not fail. All must be silent that night, and no one must leave their sleeping house for any reason whatsoever."

"We promise!" cried the people and went about getting a supply of food. They found calabashes big enough for even a pig or a dog and prayed to Niolopua, god of sleep, to help them through the night.

The night of the full moon came. Hāhālua heard the sound of humming voices and drums beating a walking cadence and the shrill sound of nose flutes. The Menehune were coming. She was curious to see them at work, but she knew the price of her curiosity, so she played kōnane with her attendants, concentrating on the black and white stones so completely that in time she forgot the work going on outside her house. In this way she passed her time.

Papaʻenaʻena formed two groups of workers. The smaller group brought stones from the beach of Makaliʻi and built a dam across a loop on the south shore. Long before the night was over, the fishpond was complete and the workers went to help the others in their greater task.

The larger group needed to bring stones from as far away as Wahiawa, almost twenty miles away. Papaʻenaʻena lined up his workers so that they stood facing one another in a staggered manner. Whenever a rock was picked up, it was handed to the first man in the file. This man in turn passed the stone to the man in the other line. In this way, each stone zigzagged from man to man from Wahiawa to Nāwiliwili. There the master builders received the stone and placed it in the wall During that night the flow of stones never stopped or faltered. Slowly the dam grew.

The Menehune built a wall almost half a mile long, eight to ten feet wide and four to ten feet high. Each stone was carefully placed over a core of tamped-down dirt.

The night was the longest Manō could remember. The moon did not seem to be moving. He heard the murmuring of voices and wanted to see the speakers. He heard the beat of the drum and longed to work to its rhythm. He heard the sound of the stones being placed and wanted to learn the craft of stone-fitting. He was filled with questions. Were they building the dam in the right place? Would it be strong enough to withstand the flooding that came with storms?

Manō paced back and forth in his house, and to him it became smaller and smaller. He felt trapped, a prisoner. Little by little he persuaded himself that he could poke a little hole through the thatching of the wall and peak outside to see what was going on, and no one would know.

Not long before dawn, that is what he did.

Papaʻenaʻena knew immediately when the chief poked his finger through the wall of his house. The Menehune commander ordered his people to drop their stones and to gather together. The men had been working with lava rock all night long, and every one of them had cut, bleeding hands. One by one they came to the nearly completed fishpond and washed their hands.

The water turned red, and the morning breeze rippled the reddened water.

There were only ten feet more to go before the dam would be finished. But the chief had broken his promise. The Menehune left the dam and never returned.

Later that day, Hāhālua, after inspecting her new fishpond and giving instructions for its use, went across the river to visit her brother. She gazed in wonder at the nearly two thousand-foot wall and sighed as she looked at the blood-red ripples.

"From now on, I shall call you ʻAlekoko, Bloody-ripple," she told her brother. "That will remind you that chiefs must always keep their word. A chief's word is law, even to that chief who says it."

From then on, Hāhālua and ʻAlekoko lived peacefully together. There were no more contests between them. ʻAlekoko only had to look at his sister's fishpond and at his own to know he had already lost.

In time, brother and sister passed away, but whenever a rainbow hovered over the river, people knew they were returning to visit. So, when a shark swam up the river to the large fishpond, people knew it was ʻAlekoko himself, and when a manta ray swam upriver, the people said that it was Hāhālua herself who had come.

"These are our vigilant chiefs," the people said and were glad.

Hiku a me Kāwelu

Keahuʻolu was his father and Lanihau was his mother, the parents of Hiku i ka nahele. Keahuʻolu was the chief of Puʻukāpele, the mountain village of the paddle makers. It was Keahuʻolu who decided when to plant koa seedlings, for these trees with crescent-moon leaves were farmed here to provide hundred-foot-long ocean-going canoes. Kauila trees, whose hard red wood was best for canoe paddles and the farmer's ʻoʻo, digging stick, were cared for here, too. From first planting to final cutting, it was Chief Keahuʻolu who led all the necessary prayers to the gods.

Hiku i ka nahele grew up in the forests of Puʻukāpele, a handsome boy, with a back as straight as a pali, a cliff that plunged into the nearby canyon. With his friends and guardians, he shouted into the huge canyon, laughing to hear his echo return to him. He often went with the birdcatchers into the lehua forests and the swamps to catch the gaily feathered honeycreepers.

His mother taught him all she knew of the plants of the uplands, their uses for canoes, paddles, digging sticks, medicines, and fragrance.

The priests taught him the prayers that one must offer the gods at the right times, the prayers to Kū, god of the forest, and to Kāne, the god of farming.

The chiefs, each of whom considered themselves Hiku's special kahu, guardian, taught the boy all that a chief must know: the physical skills of a warrior, the mental arts of an orator and chanter, the intricate skills to rule his people some day with wisdom.

Hiku, when he was little, was always getting lost in the forest, for he seldom paid any attention to where he was going. His father worried since Hiku could easily fall over a cliff, fall out of a tree. Keahuʻolu's imagination could think of many dire things that could happen. So Lanihau, although not worried at all about her son, but with far deeper reasons than her husband knew, cut a straight branch of kauila wood, which she polished into a spear. It had a blunt point on one end and a tuft of green-gold feathers on the other. Only Hiku could throw this spear. Everyone else found it too heavy.

"Throw this and follow its flight," Lanihau told Hiku. "It will always take you to your heart's desire."

"But how will I find it if I throw it in the forest?" Hiku asked.

"If you cannot see it," Lanihau replied, "then call it by name, Puanē, and it will answer you."

Hiku laughed. "A spear cannot talk," he said.

"Try it," answered his mother. "Throw it and call it by name."

So Hiku brought the spear to his shoulder, grasped it firmly, and threw it as far as he could. The spear sailed past a koa and a kauila and passed through a pūkiawe shrub, and Hiku could no longer see the spear at all.

"Puanē!" he called, expecting no answer.

But from the pūkiawe bush, the spear answered, "Nē!" Hiku ran to it and picked it up.

"Always follow Puanē," Lanihau said. Hiku promised.

Since his heart's desire was to be fed, warm, and comfortable at home, his father Keahu'olu was greatly pleased, for Hiku always returned home where food was waiting for him, and his soft bed of lauhala mats waited for him and a crackling fire warmed him during the cold nights.

By the time he changed from boy to man, there was no one who could compare with Hiku in the symmetry of his form, his athletic abilities, his skill of chanting, his knowledge of the intricate rules that govern the relationships between people, or the gentleness of his manner.

Once in awhile he gazed down the ridges that sloped gently nearly three thousand feet to the blue ocean between the islands of Kaua'i and Ni'ihau. He had never gone down to the sea. Sometimes he heard the beat of the waves breaking along the shore and wondered what surf looked like, but then a bird would call and the wind would rustle the leaves of the forest and the love of his mountains would fill him, and he forgot the sea. There was nothing there to interest him and his parents were content to have it so.

One day, Hiku threw Puanē in front of him, intending to head to Halemanu to see how the birdcatchers were faring. However Puanē led him to the top of Ke-ahu-o-Ola, a hill below their home at Pu'ukāpele, with a fine view over the tree tops down the slopes to the sea. Hiku heard a noise like the flapping wings of many birds, but he could see no flock of birds that could possibly be making that sound.

Just then, his mother joined him on top of the hill. "What is that noise, Lanihau?" he asked.

They listened as the strange sound once again rose from the beach and echoed in the mountain gulches. "Ē, Hiku," his mother said, "that is a large number of men and women on the beach clapping their hands together. The people who live by the sea are very pleased with something they are watching and they are expressing their delight. Undoubtedly some great chief or chiefess is doing something quite wonderful."

"And what is this chief or chiefess doing?" Hiku asked.

"Perhaps surfing. Perhaps something else, I do not know," Lanihau said.

"I think I shall go down to the sea," Hiku said and, picking up his spear Puanē, he ran down to the lowlands.

He came to the dunes of Pōki'i where the young people of the area had built themselves a great hālau, a shed built of hau branches and thatched with woven coconut fronds. Here, a group of young men was playing the game of ke'a pua, in which a spear made from a sugar cane tassel was thrown along the ground, and the winner was he whose spear flew the farthest.

Hiku stood leaning on his spear Puanē watching the ke'a pua players. Several young men were playing. They spent much time inspecting their spears, but, Hiku decided, they were really more interested in the young women sitting beneath the trees. One young woman in particular caught Hiku's attention. She was beautiful. She was without a blemish and was obviously of very high rank, for she had a kahu who sat beside her waving a feather kahili to chase away the flies and heat.

The game itself did not seem difficult to him. What was difficult, however, was knowing how to ask to enter the game. Hiku had never had playmates his own age and he did not know what to say. All his desires and wants had been provided for him, even before he had really thought much about what it was he wanted. Now he wanted to enter this game. He, too, hoped the young woman would notice him and smile at him.

As he gazed at her, she looked directly at him, "Perhaps you would like to play," she said. The players turned in surprise. They had not seen Hiku.

"Join us," invited one player, motioning to Hiku to come forward.

"Line up," the player ordered. "Throw your spears."

One by one the players stood at the marker and threw their spears. The spears skimmed the ground, flew up over the mound, and soared for a moment before falling into the sand.

At last it was Hiku's turn. He whispered to Puanē, "Don't fail me!" He drew back his arm and threw with all his might. The spear flew into the air and fell to earth just in front of the young woman Hiku admired.

There was much commotion, for everyone had been afraid the spear would strike the young woman. No one noticed that she picked up the spear and hid it under the mat where her attendant sat.

She watched happily as Hiku walked toward her. She had never seen a man so handsome and admired the grace with which he walked. Hiku, for his part, had never dreamed of such beauty as marked the young woman who already was smiling a welcome at him.

"I am Hiku," he announced as he stopped before her.

"I am Kāwelu," she answered.

"I think my spear dropped here," he said.

"I have not seen your spear," she replied.

Hiku said, " If I call it by name, it will answer me."

"Then call it by name."

"Puanē! Puanē!" Hiku called.

"Nē!" answered the spear.

"There you are," Hiku said to Kāwelu. "You have hidden my spear."

"Indeed," Kāwelu said. "Then come and get your spear."

As Hiku came nearer and reached for his spear, Kāwelu took off the wreath of rare and fragrant flowers she was wearing and threw it around his shoulders. This was the token to all the people that she had taken Hiku to be her husband. And so it was that Puanē, as his mother Lanihau had intended, brought Hiku to his heart's desire.

The people cheered. Kāwelu was the daughter of a chief, and had been raised carefully, protected and perfected in all the arts needed by a high chiefess. Now she had found a young husband equal to her in rank and beauty. Hiku and Kāwelu were the most beautiful beings the people had ever seen, and they believed that these two would make glad each other's lives. And they were content.

For five days they lived together in the mua, a house where both men and women could be together. They played guessing games and kōnane, sometimes shared their songs and genealogies and told marvelous stories of the sea and forest. Each day, Kāwelu left Hiku in the mua for a time to go to the women's eating house to take some food. Not once did it occur to her to offer Hiku some food and Hiku, who for all his life had found food always set out for him, never thought to ask or go find it for himself.

By the sixth evening, Hiku was very hungry and very angry. He left the mua. He said to Kāwelu's attendant, "Tell Kāwelu I am gone. I will no longer suffer the humiliation. She says she loves me, yet she will not offer me the hospitality of food. She thinks only of herself."

He began climbing the road to Puʻukāpele. The sun set in the ocean beyond Polihale, beyond the undersea domain of Milu where the dead continue their existence, and soon only the light of a crescent moon lit the path.

On her return from eating, Kāwelu found the mua empty. "Where is Hiku?" she asked her attendant.

The attendant pointed up the mountain path.

Kāwelu ran after Hiku but he was moving very fast. "Hiku!" she called. "Come back! Return to me!"

"No!" replied Hiku angrily. "I will not return. I was hungry in your house. Go back. Do not follow me!"

He turned his back on Kāwelu and ran up the path. The leaves of all the upland trees rustled loudly, greeting his return. The night birds circled above his head, hastening him on his way.

Kāwelu heard his footsteps echoing from the hills. She followed, calling,

> *O Hiku, my beloved!*
> *This ridge is steep and hard to climb*
> *O my love, wait for Kāwelu!*

Hiku refused to listen. He asked the thick fog and rainy mist to gather around Kāwelu, to force her to go back. But she struggled on through the ferns and slippery rocks. Tears, mingling with the rain, streamed down her cheeks. The fog and mist soaked her kihei, the kapa mantle which she had thrown about her shoulders as she hurried from her home after Hiku, and it began to tear.

Now in rags, chilled and shivering, she called again.

Raindrops walk on the leaves,
Beating them to the ground.
I, too, am being pressed down by the rain.
O Hiku, wait for me!

Hiku still refused to listen. He asked the plants of the forest to help him. ʻIeʻie and maile vines began to creep over the path. The ʻōhia trees drooped their branches to hinder Kāwelu's way. She continued to push through this growth, but as she struggled forward step by step, she stumbled and fell again and again into the cold wet mass of ferns and vines and into the mud and stones. She was bruised and sore and she was bleeding from the many scratches. The vines crept up around her legs and her arms and held her, but she tore them loose and forced her way upward, always calling, "Hiku, wait for me!"

But there was no answer from above. Kāwelu could no longer hear Hiku's footsteps. She wept bitter tears to find herself abandoned, for she did not understand why. She fell to her knees and again she called to him. There was only silence. Hiku was gone. Kāwelu wept.

No answer? Hiku is gone.
Kāwelu shall follow the Koʻolau wind over the sea
And string the blossoms of the kou tree
In the land of Pō with Milu as my companion.
Shall I remember Hiku below?
Farewell then. Remember me.

Kāwelu, wet, bleeding, despairing, returned to her village. She stood at the door of the house where she had been so happy with Hiku. She said to her attendant, "I am going to sleep now and I don't want you to wake me up or to come in, even if you hear noises. I shall awaken and come out only when I feel like it."

She entered the house and taking a piece of ʻieʻie vine, she wound one end about a rafter and, stepping on an upturned calabash, wound the other end around her throat.

The beautiful chiefess died. As her body gradually became lifeless, her soul crept upward to the luaʻuhane, the little hole in the corner of the eye, the door by which the soul passes out of the body into the ghostly world. Kāwelu's spirit slowly and sadly began to journey to Pō, the undersea world of the dead.

After a full day had gone by, her attendant became restless and a little worried about Kāwelu. At last, she opened the door of the house and saw Kāwelu hanging from the ceiling. Her people mourned Kāwelu for many days, for they had all loved their chiefess.

When their first mourning was over, they went into the mountains to gather ʻieʻie vines to weave into a kāʻai, a special basket into which they would place the bones of Kāwelu. They went past Puʻukāpele into the deep forest. They wailed when they returned in the late afternoon, mourning the death of their beloved chiefess.

Lanihau came to the edge of the path and asked them why they had come and why they wailed.

"We came for ʻieʻie vine to prepare a casket for our chiefess who is dead," they replied.

"What is her name?" asked Lanihau. "Perhaps she is a relative of mine."

"Her name is Kāwelu," came the answer. "Her husband left her and she followed him but he would not return with her. So she came back alone and hung herself in her house."

"I weep with you," replied Lanihau.

She stood there under a koa tree until the mourners had gone out of sight on their home-ward journey. She stood and waited until her son Hiku returned.

Hiku had once again fallen under the spell of his beloved forest. The brightly feathered honeycreepers flew with him as he ran under the heavily shaded depths of the trees. He ran with the winds and the storms as they raged in the mountains. He was happy to breathe again the cool air which surrounded him throughout his childhood. If he thought of Kāwelu at all, it was to think of her at home or under the shade of the kou trees, and someday, he thought, he would go back to the shore and see her again.

When evening fell, Hiku returned home. His mother stopped him.

"Kāwelu is dead," she told Hiku. "Didn't you hear the mourners wailing in the mountains? They came to gather ʻieʻie vine to weave a kāʻai for her bones."

Hiku burst into tears. "I did not think she was ill."

"She was not," Lanihau said. "Her husband, they say, deserted her and she killed herself in her sorrow. And you were that husband, were you not, Hiku?"

Hiku nodded, tears streaming down his face, his heart aching with loss.

"Why did you leave?" Lanihau demanded.

"I stayed with her five days," Hiku said. "Not once did she give me something to eat."

"Why did you not ask for food? Why did you not go out to the men's eating house and feed yourself?" Lanihau asked.

Hiku looked at her in astonishment. "I did not think of it," he said.

"Then yours is the blame," his mother said. She told him how thoughtless and heedless he had been to desert Kāwelu as he did and not to answer her chants. Hiku was overcome with grief.

"What can I do?" Hiku said. "I would do anything to bring her back to life and take care of her and undo the injury I have caused her."

"Then, my son," said Lanihau, "go to the heiau of Polihale and ask the kahuna nui, the high priest, what you must do to regain the spirit of Kāwelu and restore her to life."

Hiku went to Polihale. The kahuna nui, Hulumānienie, spread his offerings on the altar. "You must know," Hulumānienie said, "that the spirits of the dead go to the underworld, to the dark and gloomy land of Milu. There they play their favorite games and time passes slowly and soon they forget their earthly life. There is where the spirit of Kāwelu is.

"The god Lolupe, he who punishes after death those who have spoken ill of the king, and yet protects those who are not guilty of any law-breaking, tells me that although he has taken Kāwelu to Milu, he keeps her safe. Her body here on earth remains as though she were in a deep sleep, not in death. She can be restored to life, but only by someone willing to risk his own.

"Few living men have ever gone to the land of Milu. If the ghost warriors of Milu find you there, they will capture you and punish you with the worst tortures they can think of and you will never again return to the upper world. Yet you must go there and capture her soul and return it to her body. Will you do this? "

"Yes," Hiku answered. "It is my fault Kāwelu's spirit is with Milu. Whatever I must do, I will do."

"Good," said Hulumānienie. "Now, first you must make a container out of two halves of a coconut shell. The edges must fit so tightly that it is watertight. You must make this container yourself. No one else can do it for you. Bring it to me when you are done."

Hiku went to the coconut grove of Kaunalewa and found a coconut shell and carefully cut it in half. He burnished the entire shell until, when the halves were fitted together, no water seeped through. This he brought to Hulumānienie who nodded approvingly.

"Now," said the kahuna nui, "you must weave yourself a long, long rope of the invisible vine, long enough to reach Ka-lua-o-Milu. When that is done, return to me."

"May I have help in making this rope?" Hiku asked.

"Yes," answered Hulumānienie. "One man cannot do this alone."

So Hiku gathered his friends in the mountains and they searched in every valley for olonā plants. These they pounded and twisted and wove a long rope, long enough, they thought, to reach Ka-lua-o-Milu. When Hiku brought this to Hulumānienie, the kahuna nui shook his head. "Olonā is not the invisible vine," he said. "Try again."

Now Hiku went to the seashore and asked the friends of Kāwelu to help him. Together they gathered long strands of the koali vine. These they wove into a long stout rope which Hiku took back to the kahuna nui of Polihale heiau.

Hulumānienie shook his head. "This is not the invisible vine," he said. "Try again."

Thoroughly discouraged, Hiku left the heiau grounds and walked along the sand dunes. What else could he use to weave a rope that would help him rescue Kāwelu? He dragged his feet in the sand, sad and weary. Suddenly he tripped and fell. Looking about he saw a green leaf sticking up out of the sand and near it a small white flower blossomed. Hiku smiled with relief. This was the hunakai vine, which never showed itself completely. "This is the invisible vine," Hiku called to his friends in the mountains and to Kāwelu's friends on the shore. "Help me to weave a rope to rescue Kāwelu!"

Men gathered hunakai along the dunes from Polihale to Waimea. Women braided three strands together, making a rope that stretched from one end of the beach to the other. Then they all went with Hiku back to Polihale and showed Hulumānienie what they had made.

The kahuna nui nodded. "Good," he said. "Now you must get a canoe and some men and row out over Ka-lua-o-Milu. Then you must make a loop at one end of this rope to act as a seat where you will sit and your friends will lower you until you come to the bottom. Find Kāwelu, capture her soul in the coconut container, and return. Go to where the body of Kāwelu waits and entice her spirit to enter the body and she will return to life. But remember, if the ghostly warriors realize you are a living man, they will capture you and never again will you see the light of day. Is all clear to you?"

"Yes," said Hiku. He borrowed a large canoe, chose strong men to crew it, and loaded the hunakai rope on board. The canoe was launched and paddled above Ka-lua-o-Milu. Seating himself in the loop at one end of the rope, Hiku told his men, "Let me down slowly. I will jerk once on the rope to let you know I have reached bottom. After that, hang tight for if you let go, I surely shall not return. No matter how the rope moves, do not pull it up until you feel two jerks, for that will be my signal to pull me up again."

Hiku rubbed a mixture of rancid coconut and kukui oil on himself which gave him a strong, offensive odor, tied the coconut container onto his malo, and jumped into the water. Down, down, down he went and just before he thought his lungs would burst for want of air, he broke through into a great chamber.

The light was very dim but he could pick out groups of spirits playing or watching games. Hiku climbed off his rope and tied it to a rock. Then he walked from group to group, searching for Kāwelu. She was not playing kōnane, nor betting on the fighting roosters or riddling.

As he stood at the edge of each group, the spirits nearest him would move away, holding their noses. "What a bad smelling spirit!" grumbled one. Hiku knew that the strong odor of the rotten oil smeared on his skin was protecting him. No one would want to touch him and so discover that he was of living flesh.

At last he found Kāwelu. She was at the side of Milu, ruler of the underworld. He had seen Kāwelu as she had entered his realm and he had sent his ghost warriors to welcome her to Pō with great rejoicing, for she was as beautiful and royal as anyone who had ever entered the realm of the dead. Milu was listening to Kāwelu as she sang her family song. This was the song that had been composed at her birth, and it was sung by any chief or chiefess whenever she visited another chief far away from her own home.

When she had finished, she began a chant which she and Hiku had composed themselves in their few days together. Kāwelu sang the first part and where Hiku had chanted the response, her voice faltered.

Suddenly from the throng of ghosts which surrounded them rose the sound of a clear voice chanting the response, which only Hiku could know.

Kāwelu, who had not been dead for so long that she had forgotten all that had happened to her while alive, was overcome by the thought that Hiku, too, was dead and now among the ghosts. She looked around the crowd but did not see Hiku. Her shoulders slumped and she threw her kihei over her shoulders and wandered away. The ghosts, at a signal from Milu, let her go and did not follow her.

Kāwelu roamed from place to place, looking for Hiku. Sometimes she softly chanted her part of their song. Once she heard a whispered reply but the only ghost near her was a foul smelling, dirt-covered ghost. She turned away from him in despair. Again she heard the faint whisper and followed it.

She came to the rock where Hiku had tied his rope. The foul smelling ghost was there, sitting on a stick fastened at the end of the rope. The ghost began to swing back and forth, back and forth. Sometimes he pushed his feet against the ground to swing high and sometimes he braked his motion by dragging his feet against the ground.

One ghost called out to him, "Ē, you awful-smelling spirit, can I do that, too?"

Hiku stopped the swing. "Certainly," he said. "Try it."

Hiku held the swing while the ghost climbed on. The ghost kicked his feet against the ground but, having forgotten to hold onto the rope, fell backwards to the ground.

Hiku chanted.

> *I have a swing,*
> *While the rest of you children do not.*
> *When you fall, it is only to sit on your behind!*

All the ghosts laughed. They thought it was a great joke. Everyone wanted to jump on the rope and swing. One by one they tried and fell until the whole crowd was chanting Hiku's song.

Hiku approached Kāwelu. "Here is a swing. Come ride with me."

"I won't ride with you," Kāwelu replied. "You smell too awful. Besides I will only fall like the rest."

"I can sit on the swing," Hiku said, "and you can cover me with your kihei and sit in my lap. Then we will swing together."

Kāwelu agreed. The ghosts thought this new arrangement was amusing and they shouted approval. Hiku took the spirit of Kāwelu in his strong arms and began to swing slowly back and forth. Then he pushed faster and faster and they sailed higher and higher until the ghosts below marvelled at how fast and far they were going. Hiku jerked on his rope twice and the swing began to rise toward the dome of the cavern.

Before long, however, it dawned on one of the ghosts below that the swing was higher than before and Hiku no longer touched the ground with his feet. "He is stealing the woman!" cried the ghost. "He is stealing the woman!"

All the ghosts in the underworld yelled and shouted, and the noise echoed throughout the cavern. Some of the ghosts leaped into the air, trying to catch Hiku's feet, others called out to him to return, and others began muttering charms to cause his downfall. But no one could leap high enough, and Hiku had no intention of returning, and the curses did not work. The swing was being drawn higher and higher.

As they neared the roof of the cavern, Kāwelu's spirit began to shrink. She became the size of a child, then the size of a doll, and then the size of a butterfly. Just before they burst through the roof into the deep ocean, Hiku caught Kāwelu's spirit and enclosed it in the coconut container. It sealed so tightly that no water could enter Kāwelu's prison.

Hiku's friends pulled Hiku into the canoe and they sped to shore. Hiku rushed to the house where the body of his greatly loved Kāwelu still lay as though she were sleeping. Hiku kneeled at her feet, and uttered a prayer to Lolupe. Then he cut a hole in the big toe of her left foot and with great difficulty and many prayers forced the spirit of Kāwelu out of the container and into the wound, for the soul must travel from the feet to the eyes on its return. The spirit struggled desperately, for the body was cold. Hiku began to lomilomi, rubbing the flesh back to warmth, working the spirit farther and farther into the body.

Once the soul reached Kāwelu's heart, her blood began to flow again and her lungs began to breathe. The spirit spread through her body and Kāwelu opened her eyes and saw Hiku bending lovingly over her.

"How could you be so cruel as to leave me?" she murmured.

"Never again," promised Hiku and he hugged the woman he loved so much that he had dared to challenge the ghosts of the dead to bring her back to him.

From then on, there were no more troubles in the lives of Hiku and Kāwelu. In the cool months they lived by the sea and when it was hot they lived in the forests. They could never be separated.

Even after they went back to Ka-lua-o-Milu at the time appointed to them, they could not be separated and would remain together until the world itself ceased to exist.

Māmā-akua-Lono

They skimmed the waves from Rai'atea of the southern seas on their red-sailed voyaging canoe, seeking the island of Kaua'i. Niolopua, god of sleep, and his family were searching for the silent Mū people, the very first settlers of this land.

"They're not doing very well," Lono, god of agriculture, had told him. "Find them, and help them. The gods of the ocean tides shall go with you, Keaumiki, the ebbing tide, and Keaukā, the swelling tide. They shall guard you on your long voyage."

Niolopua obeyed, and with his wife, Hina, his sister, Māmā-akua-Lono, and his two younger brothers, 'Ūlili, the wandering tattler, and Kōlea, the golden plover, he set sail across the deep blue sea.

Each evening, Māmā-akua-Lono took up a piece of 'awa root and chewed it, spitting out the pulp into a small calabash. When there was enough, she mixed the pulp with rain water, strained the liquid through a fiber sieve and poured a few drops over the side of the canoe, an offering to Lono. Then she filled a polished coconut cup for her brother. He drank the bitter juice, ate a piece of sugar cane, and lay down to sleep. Then men and women on their beds of lauhala mats also fell asleep and shared in the pleasant dreams of Niolopua.

Hina's dreams were troubled. She had nothing to do. Māmā-akua-Lono prepared the 'awa; her brothers could fly freely from the confining canoe. Her husband Niolopua never consulted her about their lives and indeed seldom spoke to her. Hina was unhappy and soon came to dislike Māmā-akua-Lono.

During the day the younger brothers changed into their bird forms and flew away from the canoe searching for Kaua'i. 'Ūlili, the gray-striped wandering tattler, and Kōlea, the golden-spotted plover, flew far ahead of the canoe. Day after day they searched the restless ocean, while Keaumiki and Keaukā kept storms away and calmed the wind and waves so that Niolopua and his family were not drenched with salt spray.

Hina remained inside, made deathly ill by the slightest motion of the canoe. She wanted to

Māmā-akua-Lono ⤛

return to her homeland. She heard her husband speak gently to his sister and thought that he never spoke to her with that gentleness in his voice. Her dislike grew.

One afternoon, ʻŪlili came skimming across the wave tops and settled on his sister's shoulder. Māmā-akua-Lono chanted:

> ʻŪlili, ʻŪlili, wandering tattler,
> Pecking on the sea's shore,
> What did you see?

"There is an island ahead," ʻŪlili piped. "It is surrounded by many long white beaches. There are reefs filled with good things to eat. There is a mighty river mouth just ahead of us and a surf made for the sport of heʻe nalu, sliding down waves."

"Are the Mū there?" Niolopua asked.

"I did not see them," ʻŪlili replied.

"I have!" Kōlea yelled as he lit on the other shoulder of his sister.

Māmā-akua-Lono chanted to him:

> Kōlea, Kōlea, migrating plover,
> Drinking from the mountain springs,
> What did you see?

"To the north there is a round island, with many rivers and waterfalls and thick forests and gleaming white beaches. No island I have ever seen is as beautiful."

"And the Mū?" Māmā-akua-Lono asked.

"I have seen them," said Kōlea. "They live in the mountain valleys and they eat bananas. Their houses are covered with banana leaves and they dress themselves in banana leaves."

"Lead the way to Kauaʻi, then," Niolopua said. Kōlea launched himself up, yelling to ʻŪlili to join him, and the brothers flew in front of the voyaging canoe. The wind freshened, the red sail billowed out, and the canoe swam across the waves.

The canoe kept its speed as it neared the land of Wailua. The vessel sped down the crest of a wave and swept into the river mouth. Finally, just after the river split into two parts, the canoe gently beached itself below a steep cliff where there were three caves.

"We are home," Niolopua said. "Hina and I shall make our home in the highest cave, near the crest of that cliff. The cliff's name shall be Maunakapu, Sacred Mountain, home of Niolopua, god of sleep."

Niolopua brought sleep and pleasant dreams to men and women at night and by day helped the Mū as Lono had asked. He taught them to build house frames on which to hang their woven mats of banana leaves. He taught them to line the floor with ferns so they would be warm and comfortable at nights. He was busy and so were ʻŪlili and Kōlea, messengers flying far and wide, telling their brother and sister the news of all they saw.

Māmā-akua-Lono built her house inside the large cave just above the river. Long fronds of fern hung down over the opening, screening her from the hot rays of the sun and the disturbing light of the moon.

Below her house, a tall lehua tree leaned over the river. Its flowers were reflected in the clear water, and it seemed to all who saw it that there were two trees there, sharing the same roots. Māmā-akua-Lono sat under this tree every day with her kapa anvil of hard red milo wood resting in front of her. Within easy reach of her right hand she placed an array of kapa beaters, each carved with intricate patterns by her brother Niolopua. Within easy reach of her left hand was an array of dyes in gourds and coconut pots, and bamboo sticks with patterns carved into the ends of them by her other brothers, Kōlea and ʻŪlili.

From far and wide, the Mū came to the cave of Māmā-akua-Lono. They traded for a sheet of her kapa, more comfortable as clothing than the banana leaves they used. They bartered bunches of mountain bananas, wild taro, fresh fish, and sometimes a necklace of brightly colored sea shells. Māmā-akua-Lono offered to show them how to make kapa of their own. Soon she was surrounded by a group of chattering women.

Only Hina was not happy. She missed her former home. From her house, Hina could watch Māmā-akua-Lono at work. She became envious of the many gifts brought to Māmā-akua-Lono as she sat beneath her lehua tree. She hated being alone. If only the Mū women would come to her. But she was never asked to join the chattering group.

One night, Hina woke her husband up and said, "Tell your sister to give me something to do."

Yawning, Niolopua went to his sister. "Please give my wife something to do," he said.

"Would she like to learn to beat kapa?" Māmā-akua-Lono asked.

"I think so," Niolopua said, too sleepy to think clearly.

"Then give her this strip of wauke bark," said the sister. "I have cleaned it, and it is ready for her to beat out."

Hina, however, had never beaten kapa. It was something other women, not someone like herself, the wife of a god, did. She wanted to join Māmā-akua-Lono under the lehua tree so she could talk to the Mū people when they came along. Hina thought Māmā-akua-Lono was insulting her, for she certainly should know that Hina did not know anything about making kapa.

The more she thought, twisting the strip of kapa in her hands, shredding it into little pieces, the angrier Hina became.

Niolopua was sound asleep. Kōlea and 'Ūlili were flying here and there, spying out the events in all the villages of Kaua'i. There was no one to stop Hina from her plan, for she too had a certain gift. During that night, she built a high dam across the river just below the junction. The water backed up and began to climb higher and higher up the mountainsides.

At dawn, Māmā-akua-Lono awoke and saw that the water was already creeping into her cave. The only way she could escape was to swim. She waded into the water, and, with quick strokes, she set out for the upper side of the large lake that had completely drowned the lehua tree.

As soon as Māmā-akua-Lono reached the middle of the lake, Hina broke the dam and the young woman was washed out to sea in the flood.

Kōlea saw the flood roaring down to the sea. He called to his brother 'Ūlili, "Come quickly, and see!"

'Ūlili gasped. "A flood? I have never seen that before. How did it happen? It didn't rain last night."

"Never mind that," Kōlea said excitedly. "Isn't that someone being carried out to sea by the flood?"

"Yes, it is our sister," 'Ūlili said, and the brothers flew out over the ocean. They began to weep as they saw their sister, for there was no way they could save her. Their bird forms were too small to pick her out of the water.

'Ūlili said, "Kōlea, wake up our brother. He can save her. I will stay here above our sister so there will be no mistaking where she is."

Kōlea flew home to find his brother faster than he had ever flown before.

Hina was waiting outside the house. "No, do not wake him. He especially told me no one must wake him today."

Kōlea flitted past her and shook Niolopua by the shoulder. "Quickly, quickly, or our sister will be lost."

Niolopua rushed to the top of Maunakapu. He saw the traces of the flood. He saw that the lehua tree where his sister had sat was dropping its flowers one by one, and in a row these blossoms were floating down the river, following Māmā-akua-Lono out to sea.

Māmā-akua-Lono was sure she would drown. 'Ūlili flew above her head but there was nothing he could do. Love for her brothers welled up, and, treading water, she chanted.

> *Farewell to you, Niolopua, my brother.*
> *As you wander the sleeping land,*
> *Dream of Māmā-akua-Lono.*
> *As you fly to distant lands, 'Ūlili,*
> *Think of Māmā-akua-Lono.*
> *As you flit from place to place,*
> *Kōlea, golden plover, seeking the news,*
> *Do not seek Māmā-akua-Lono.*
> *Farewell!*

Niolopua heard his sister's voice and listened to her lament. Then he, too, chanted.

> *I am Niolopua, the brother,*
> *We two dwelt on the hillside of Maunakapu.*
> *You released our brothers the birds*
> *To seek a trail across the ocean swells —*
> *Kōlea, who went to the mountain water sources,*
> *'Ūlili who pecks at the sea foam,*
> *Swimming together to the open spaces;*
> *What would I have done without your affection?*

I am a lei without the brow to wear it.
My brow is bent over with humiliation;
My body is filled with endless sorrow.

All Niolopua could do to help his sister was to put her to sleep so that she would no longer be aware of the death that was coming to her.

'Ūlili and Kōlea circled above her, their wailing cries echoing from the curling waves. This sound reached the ears of Lono and he looked out and saw the woman who faithfully chewed a cup of 'awa for him every day. He gestured and the sea and the creatures that live in it obeyed. Keaumiki and Keaukā rose to the surface of the sea and took Māmā-akua-Lono in their arms. The waves gentled and rocked her as a mother rocks her baby. The porpoises came and guarded Māmā-akua-Lono through the long days and nights.

Māmā-akua-Lono never knew how long she floated in the ocean, passing O'ahu and Moloka'i and Lāna'i until she reached the shore of Maui. Here she crawled across the beach and crept among the pōhuehue vines. Warmed by the sun, she fell asleep again.

The sisters of Chief Moku'ula, as they did every day, walked along the beach gathering strands of pōhuehue vine which they would weave into a stiff and uncomfortable dress for themselves and a loincloth for their brother. They knew nothing of kapa even though wauke trees grew near their homes. On this day, one of them saw something brown among the pōhuehue vines. They pulled apart the web of vines and saw that a woman was lying there.

"I wonder if she is pretty?" the older sister said.

The other said, hesitating, "Maybe her back is good looking and her face is ugly."

"Let's find out," replied the other. She shook the shoulder of the sleeping young woman. "Wake up," she said. "Wake up."

Māmā-akua-Lono sat up. The two women stared at her critically. They saw no blemish of any kind nor any disfigurement. Her face was as beautiful as the full moon. Her back was as straight as the black cliffs that plunge into the ocean.

"My brother Moku'ula is without a wife," the older sister said.

"Would you care to be his wife? And our friend?" said the younger shyly. "We would like that."

Māmā-akua-Lono accepted. It was for this, perhaps, that she had been saved by Keaumiki and Keaukā. She became the wife of Moku‘ula and friend to his sisters.

Soon after their marriage, Māmā-akua-Lono asked her husband to build a house for them and build a strong, tall fence all the way around it. Taking her sisters-in-law with her, she showed them how to plant wauke in fields high in the valley. She taught them how to strip the bark from the stalks, how to soak these strips in the stream until they were of the right consistency. She told her husband to carve a kapa beating board and showed him how to carve the beaters. Then she showed the women how to beat a strip of wauke bark into a sheet of kapa, and how to decorate it with homemade dyes and brushes of lauhala keys. At last she showed them how to make a pā‘ū, a dress for themselves, a malo, loincloth, for their brother, and how to knot two corners of kapa to make a kihei, a cloak against the chill mountain night winds.

She never revealed to the sisters how homesick she was, how she longed to see her brothers again, how much she wanted to return to her home on the banks of the Wailua river.

Day after day, Māmā-akua-Lono sat at her anvil and beat strips of wauke into kapa. The two sisters sat beside her and learned as best they could although the kapa they made was never as fine, thin, and delicate as that beaten by Māmā-akua-Lono. Little by little, the house filled with kapa pieces. Neighbors saw the sisters in their new clothes and asked how to make them, how they might obtain them. Soon Moku‘ula and his sisters were considered wealthy people, for their calabash was never empty of poi, and there was always salt to preserve the many fish they took in exchange for a piece of Māmā-akua-Lono's kapa.

The sisters began to teach their neighbors what they had learned. One day, Māmā-akua-Lono looked about her house and saw it was filled with kapa. She had repaid any debt she might owe Moku‘ula and it was time for her to go.

Early one morning she walked to the beach and, facing the wind she chanted:

> ‘Ūlili, ‘Ūlili, wandering tattler,
> Leave your feeding place on the shore!
> Kōlea, Kōlea, migrant plover,
> Leave your mountain springs to flow alone!
> Keaumiki, ebbing tide,

Keaukā, rising tide,
Come to me here.
I am ready to go home.

Soon she climbed into the canoe paddled by Keaumiki and Keaukā and ʻŪlili and Kōlea circled the canoe, trilling and piping cries of delight, until she came home again to her cave and lehua tree on the banks of the Wailua. She greeted her brother Niolopua and her sister-in-law Hina.

"Forgive me," she said to Hina. " I did not share with you and that was wrong."

"It is I who have wronged you," said Hina. "I am ashamed. I will go away."

"No, stay. Let us share our tasks and duties and our pastimes and become friends." Māmā-akua-Lono held out her arms and the two embraced.

They became friends and when at last it was time, they left three rocks on the slopes of Maunakapu, a reminder that Niolopua, Hina and Māmā-akua-Lono once lived here.

Ka Moena Hohola o Mānā

anō lived on the dunes overlooking Poʻo-o-honu, a salt water pond protected from the sea by a sand dune built by the currents only at certain times of the year. It was a favorite bathing place for the chiefs of Mānā, and all who came to swim stopped to talk to Manō for a while for the view was superb. To the north there was the great swamp and open ponds where thousands of water birds lived. Beyond that was a row of villages tucked under the low cliffs that ended the long ridges dropping from the mountains. To the south there was only the island of Niʻihau and the open ocean. To his right and left, there was only sand, a dazzling white carpet of beach as far as the eye could see. To Manō, it looked like an immense strip of gleaming white kapa unrolling before his eyes.

Manō had been a paddler on a canoe, one of a fleet that sailed from Tahiti. A severe storm had separated the fleet, and Manō was the sole survivor of his canoe which had broken on the rocks of Kauaʻi. Manō had wandered the island and had come to Mānā and stood on Nohili, the sand dune that barks like a pack of dogs. On both sides of him stretched a dazzling white beach.

"He moena hohola o Mānā," he whispered, "the unfolding mat of Mānā," and knew he was home.

For many years he enjoyed his life at Mānā. Then one day he realized that he was aging and that he was not as strong as he had been that day when his canoe washed ashore. More and more he found himself thinking of his friends from Tahiti, and he grew homesick for the sight of them.

At last, one day a messenger arrived from the chief of Kōloa. As he shared a calabash of poi with Manō, the messenger said, "A canoe came from Hawaiʻi. Before it left, the captain said he had a question which had been asked by a man who had come ashore on that island after a storm had separated the fleet from the south. He wants to know if any similar canoe had been seen on any other island and whether anyone from it was still alive."

"Is there a name?" Manō asked.

"Yes," was the answer. "Kia lives in Kona on Hawai'i."

Manō sighed happily. Kia had been his best friend. It would be good to see him again, and Manō prepared to sail to Hawai'i and visit Kia.

He found a canoe heading for O'ahu. From O'ahu he sailed to Moloka'i, then to Maui. The trip was not an easy one. There were storms and often he had to wait until a canoe that would accept him as a passenger was ready to go.

Eventually Manō reached Kailua on Hawai'i island and found his friend Kia. Kia greeted Manō warmly and made him feel very welcome. Manō lived on Hawai'i almost a year before he became very restless. Kona was a beautiful place. It was hot, as was Mānā. It had an ocean teeming with fish, like Mānā. But there was no swamp, there were no low cliffs, only the land sweeping up to a huge peak lost in the clouds.

Worst of all, the beaches were tiny, almost disappearing before they had started. There was nothing to compare to his rolling mat, his moena hohola.

While they were having dinner one evening, Manō said, "Let's go to Kaua'i to my home."

"I'm happy here," his friend replied. "Why not live with me? Don't you enjoy it here?"

"You have made me welcome, but I love my home and my unfolding mat," Manō answered.

Kia looked at him curiously and asked, "What is this unfolding mat you are bragging about?"

Manō said, "Oh, my unfolding mat is large. One can take the mats on Hawai'i, Maui, and O'ahu all together and they could not cover my mat."

Kia sat for a while with his head down. Once he had accepted the fact that he would never return to Tahiti, that the people here in this place had lost the knowledge of building the great traveling canoes and had lost the knowledge of the guiding stars, Kia had remained and made a good life for himself. But he did not feel bound to the land, not the way Manō did, longing for his unfolding mat.

Finally Kia said, "Let's go to Kaua'i. I want to see this mat you think is so special."

The two men took Kia's small canoe and sailed for Kaua'i. They traveled many days until they came ashore at Kōloa. The next morning, Manō and Kia left early on foot. When they reached the summit of Kukui-o-Lono, Kia saw the gentle slopes of west Kaua'i spreading out before him. Kia asked, "Where is this mat you talk so much about?"

"Not here," Manō said. "Be patient. I will show it to you when we get home."

They reached Hanapēpē and Kia asked, "Is your unfolding mat here?"

Manō shook his head. "Not here. Be patient."

They crossed the Waimea River and came to the village. Kia said, "Is your unfolding mat here?"

"Not here," Manō said. "Be patient. I will show it to you when we get home."

Kia became more and more impatient. But always Manō's answer was the same. They traveled steadily, reaching Mānā on the second day, but when the sun had already set beyond Ka'ula island.

Kia said, his patience almost at an end, "Now we are at Mānā, where is your moena hohola?"

Manō laughed and said, "It is night. How can we see my unfolding mat? Wait until the sun is up. Then you can see how large it is."

Kia did not sleep well that night. He was not used to hearing the ocean roaring so close to his ears. He was not used to the wind rustling the pili grass thatch over his head. He heard the sound of raindrops and wondered, for the sky was blazing with stars, but when he stuck his head out the door, he realized the sound he heard was the sound of sand hitting the walls of the house, blown by the winds.

After the sun came up the next morning, Manō blindfolded his guest and led him to the top of the sand dunes of Nohili. Then Manō undid the blindfold and pointed Kia towards the cliffs at Polihale and said, "Here is my unfolding mat, these white sands. They extend as far as the eye can see."

Kia gazed at the beach. It was wide, so very wide between the lapping waves and the blue-flowered pōhuehue vines growing on the dunes. It was long. Kia knew it would take a long time to walk from where he stood to the dim cliffs at the other end of the beach. Yes, he thought, the beach does look like a mat unfolding before my eyes, truly a moena hohola.

Then Manō turned Kia around and pointed towards Kekaha. As far as Kia could see there was a beach of white sand where blue-green waves broke in white spray on one side and low bushes and vines crowned the dunes on the other. There was nothing to be seen but white sand.

Kia looked silently, first this way, then that. "What you say is true," he told Manō. "We do not have anything on Hawai'i that can compare to your beautiful unfolding mat. If you permit, I shall live here with you to the end of my days."

In the years before their bones were interred in the dunes they loved, Manō and Kia lived happily, content in their friendship, delighting always in the beauty of ka moena hohola o Mānā, the unfolding mat of Mānā.

Hanakā'ape

CHRISTINE FAYÉ ©97

They traveled like the wind, this procession of supernatural women, daughters of Haumea, like eddies of the air that fluttered the leaves on the kukui trees as they passed.

People saw a great procession of women all dressed in red coming along the road and ran to see them more closely. Small dust whirlwinds blew into their eyes, and later no one could say for sure that they had seen the goddess Kapo-ʻula-kīnaʻu or any of her younger sisters as they came along the road from Mānā, through Hanapēpē, across the Kalāheo uplands, and down the trail to Kōloa.

This group, laughing and chattering like the wild forest people the birdcatchers sometimes heard far up in the lonely forests, strolled along the banks of Kaʻele Stream, passing nesting pairs of piwai, the duck already doomed to extinction because its flesh was delicious and it never learned to fear man. Kapo-ʻula-kīnaʻu stopped for a moment at Maʻulili Pond, but the sun was not yet overhead and it was neither time to rest nor time to eat, so reluctantly they left the shaded pool to follow Waikomo Stream to the sea. The land grew drier, the air hotter, but before long the cool unulau, the trade winds from the northeast, tugged at the flower wreaths that hung about their necks and at the edges of their dresses, and cooled them as they passed.

They crossed over Waikomo Stream to wander down its western bank. Within the sound of the sea, Kapo stopped for a moment. Heat waves danced before them but did not form mirages as they did at Mānā. Thatched houses drowsed here and there in the heat, and there were many hālau waʻa, canoe sheds, along the shore, for fishermen had discovered that this lee side of the island was rich in fish.

Nearby a woman screamed once in pain, then again. Kapo and her group hurried around the corner of the trail. Before them was a deep, gourd-shaped bay where blue and green water surged onto rocky low cliffs. On the left a headland stretched into the sea, sheltering the bay. There was a very large hala tree on this headland that shaded a hālau waʻa. There a group of people watched a man with a stick hitting a woman crouched before him. Again and again his arm rose and fell, and at each blow the woman cried out. She rolled to the ground, curling up her legs to cover her stomach, curling her arms to protect her face, yet the man did not stop. None of the spectators looked away; none tried to stop the man or help the woman.

Kapo's anger flared. She rushed to the circle of watchers and touched the shoulder of a white-haired woman who was holding a black piglet tightly against her chest.

"Luahine, what is happening?" Kapo asked.

"Nākea is beating Lupe again," the luahine, the old woman, replied.

"Does he do this often?" Kapo demanded, her voice trembling in rage.

The old woman shrugged. "Whenever he returns without fish," she replied.

Kapo understood. Whenever a fisherman returned from a fishing expedition without fish, the gods had not helped him and the fault, never with the fisherman himself, lay on the shore. Somehow or another, the woman waiting at home was to blame. Either she had eaten a banana or she had told a neighbor that he was going fishing and the fish heard her and fled. There were many things a wife could do to offend the fishing god.

Kapo looked around the ring of spectators. There were several burly, wide-shouldered men, obviously fishing companions of Nākea, still holding nets, letting them droop onto the dirt. Near a shingle bench two boys held the rope that connected a four-man outrigger canoe to the shore. With each wave the canoe tugged at the rope and was slowly pulling itself free. There were other women, two looking up from their kapa anvils shaded by a hala tree, their beaters held silent across their knees. A girl of no more than five years, her hands over her ears, had buried her head in the lap of an older sister. Tears ran down the older girl's face.

"And why do none of you help Lupe? Why don't you stop him?" Kapo demanded.

The luahine replied, "He doesn't beat her long. It will soon stop, you'll see. Maybe this time she will learn not to be so ka'ape, so disobedient, to orders. Why should I stop him beating her? It's nothing to do with me."

The man continued to beat the woman. Everyone else was frozen in place, waiting for the beating to be over so they could go about their business again. Blood trickled from Lupe's mouth and from a cut that had opened on her shoulder. She moaned as Nākea's stick drove down on her hand-covered ear.

Kapo raged at the sight of the beating, at the indifference of the spectators, at the helplessness of the two little girls. She called upon her inner powers and summoned from where it slumbered within her that part of her being called Pua, her makani noho, a spirit that can enter into another being. Kapo gestured. Pua flew from the end of Kapo's finger and entered the body of Lupe.

Instantly Lupe, the beaten woman, turned into a dog. It was a large dog, much larger than any of those that were grown as food. It was a reddish-brown color, with a large head and massive jaws lined with sharp teeth. The spectators gasped and tried to turn and run, but Kapo, with another gesture, froze them in place with her power. Nākea struck the dog with the stick he held in his hand.

Then the brindled dog rose to its feet with a snarl and, as Nākea tried to hit it again, twisted and grabbed the stick from his hand and snapped the stick in two. The dog caught the man's hand in its jaw and instantly bloodstained the fingers. Then it was the man's scream that echoed across the bay. Nākea backed, trying to get away from the dog, but the animal, letting go of the hand, leapt for the man's chest and tore at it with paw and jaw, leaving great scratches welling with blood.

Quickly the dog leapt for the man's throat, and Nākea reeled and fell. It was his last moment in the warmth of the sun.

The luahine screeched and grabbed up a rock to throw at the dog, and the piglet kicked free of her arm and ran squealing down the road. The dog snarled, baring its red-flecked teeth and advanced upon the woman, but one of the fishermen threw a cowrie shell. The dog moved slowly away from the luahine, facing one person and then the next. Each quavered and recoiled at the dog's fierce glance.

Kapo whispered to her sister Kahalai'a, "Quickly, bring me some mahiki shrimp."

Kahalai'a went to the two boys holding the canoe.

"Where can I find mahiki shrimp?" she asked them.

"There aren't any," said one.

"I've never heard of them," said the other. Their eyes were huge with a combination of fear and excitement. The canoe tugged again and this time freed itself from the boys and began to drift in the ocean.

Kapo called out to Kahalaiʻa, "Never mind then. Get me some mahiki grass."

Kahalaiʻa obeyed and pulled up a bunch of mahiki grass she found growing in a cranny at the water's edge She took it to Kapo.

Kapo whistled. The dog bounded to her side. Kapo thrust some grass leaves into its mouth and called Pua, her supernatural self, to return to her. In this way Kapo taught that everything that grows in the ocean is matched by something growing on land, and either mahiki shrimp or mahiki grass will overcome a transformation.

The dog disappeared, and the woman stood before Kapo.

The people were free also. With a shout one of the fishermen launched himself into the sea after the canoe. The two young girls ran and held onto the hands of Lupe. The seated women rose and raised their kapa beaters threateningly over their heads.

Kapo realized that she had saved the woman from one fate only to put her life in jeopardy. These people would kill Lupe because they were frightened by what they had seen, by the body of Nākea who no longer felt the hot sun beating down on him. They must be made to realize that the goddess had spoken. Once again Kapo sent her spiritual form Pua into the woman.

Lupe's hair rose in single strands around her head, forming a black halo. Her eyes rolled up into her head, leaving the white eyeballs staring sightlessly at the advancing women. The luahine gasped and stopped, for Lupe's eyes glared at her like the mother-of-pearl eyes of the wooden images of the gods that protected their temples.

Lupe said, her voice seeming to come from a rock beside the old woman, "Luahine, beware! Your pig has run away. It will not come when you call. You must make a proper offering to Hina, wife of Kuʻula and goddess of fisher folk. You will find your pig wandering along the slippery rocks of Poʻipu. Call, and the pig will come. If you have failed to give Hina a pleasing offering, she will send the pig to the sharks waiting for it."

The luahine fell back a step. She had raised the piglet from an infant, saving it from being rolled and crushed by its impatient and bad-tempered sow. The piglet slept with her in her house and had never before wandered off. Nevertheless, the luahine would take no chances. If this prophecy were right, then this woman that she knew as Lupe was indeed inhabited by a god and must be obeyed. The offering would be given. The luahine began to plan what she would give Hina.

Lupe turned her sightless eyes upon one of the fishermen. "Today you fished in a kapu, forbidden, fishing ground," she said. "That is why you caught nothing. It is your fault, not the god's, not mine! Today the ko'a, fishing ground, is under kapu. Tomorrow the kapu will be lifted, and there you will find all the fish you can take. Do not fail to leave Ku'ula his offerings and his prayers first."

Amazed that she knew they had gone to a forbidden deep-sea fishing ground, some of the fishermen picked up Nākea's body and carried it away while others went to the hālau wa'a and began to prepare their equipment for the next day.

One of the women sitting by her kapa anvil said, "Is she possessed by the gods?"

"I will find out," the first one said. "Only someone possessed by a god can know what is inside a closed bundle. Lupe, tell me, what is in this?" The woman held up a bundle tightly wrapped in unbleached kapa.

Lupe said, "I will turn my back to you. Open your package and lift up each thing so all may see it, and I will name them."

This the woman did. There were two coconut shells containing dyes, and Lupe named the containers and the colors of the dyes. One by one the woman displayed to the others her 'ohe kāpala, bamboo stamps used to print designs on kapa, and Lupe also described the patterns carved on each. There was a mortar and pestle used for grinding bark, roots, dirt, or charcoal to powder, a gourd containing mokihana seeds for their scent, all items used in the making of kapa. Not once did Lupe hesitate. Not once did she make a mistake.

"It's true," the woman said. "Lupe is possessed by a god."

Then Lupe began to chant and dance. Her movements were like those of a puppet moved by strings and sticks, and her words were so mixed up that the two little girls laughed. At this sound, Lupe's eyes rolled forward, and her hair softened. She knelt down and hugged the little girls. Then she smiled up at Kapo.

"I do not know how to thank you," she said. "But as the evening shadows are now long, let me offer you the hospitality of my home."

That night Kapo and her maidens slept well, pleased with the hospitality of Lupe. This was the first time Kapo had entered the soul of a woman in Hawai'i, although it was certainly not the last.

The next day Kapo and her entourage continued on their journey. The goddess Keaolewa called down from her temple at the top of Hāʻupu, "Come, Kapo, you must be tired and hungry. Come up and eat and rest."

Kapo answered with truth, "No, thank you. When we return, we shall climb to the top of Hāʻupu and share your hospitality. But we have had the best that Kōloa can offer last night and we are neither tired nor hungry."

The lost pig was found on the slippery rocks with sharks waiting for it to fall. The luahine had prayed well and the piglet ran safely into her arms. The fishermen did not neglect their prayers and offerings, and the deep-sea koʻa yielded up its fish in great quantity. Never again was Lupe beaten, and from time to time she would fall into a trance and people would come from near and far to hear her prophesies, for she always spoke the truth.

The bay was named Hanakāʻape, The bay of the disobedient one, in memory of Lupe who was saved by the goddess Kapo-ʻula-kīnaʻu.

Weoweo-pilau

CHRISTINE FAYE 97©

When Lohe heard that the priests of Hale'ō'io heiau on the seashore of Kōloa had sighted a huge school of 'āweoweo, big-eyed red fish feeding on the reefs, Lohe was very happy. Lohe was a farmer who lived on the slopes of Kamo'oloa Ridge far above the sea, and he had a large family to feed. They ate well enough of the taro and sweet potatoes Lohe grew, but some fine fresh fish was always a welcome treat. Lohe was no fisherman, but he knew that when such a school feeds near shore, even the most inexperienced fisherman can easily catch all he can eat. He picked up his umeke, a gourd calabash with its tight cover, warned his wife not to eat any bananas in his absence, and set off for the Kōloa shore.

The 'āweoweo were indeed running and Lohe was able to fill his umeke with the fish in a very short time. "What a feast we will have tonight!" he thought happily. "It's been a long time since we've eaten our fill of fish." His mouth watered as he swung the full umeke over his back and started up the long road home.

He marched along humming happily. The day was pleasantly warm. It was still only late morning. He passed the village of Kōloa and came to the hill where the hōlua sledders were racing against each other down the side on their narrow sleds. Lohe wanted to watch but he felt the weight of the fish on his back and knew he had to get home with them as quickly as possible.

He continued climbing uphill, feeling rather annoyed. He loved watching hōlua racing. His wife scolded him often because he gambled on races, betting on which hōlua rider would slide to the bottom first. Was it his fault if the sledder he bet on happened to have a bad day? But then he thought of the fish again. There were four fish for each member of his family, even for his wife's mother who was sure to come for she always seemed to know when there was food in the house. Walking faster, he left the temptation of the hōlua slide behind him.

He passed into the deep shade of a grove of kukui, candlenut trees, and a voice from the darkness called out to him, "Aloha, fisherman!"

Lohe peered into the shadow and saw an old woman sitting under a tree. Her uncombed gray hair hung down over her shoulders. Her clothing of white kapa barkcloth was torn and dirty, and he thought she was wearing an old bedding sheet someone had thrown away. She was a beggar, he decided, and one never knew with beggars if they'd move into the house if there was any kindness shown or food offered; then, they could never be gotten out again. He nodded at her but kept walking.

The old woman cried out, "Wait, fisherman! Please give me some fish. You have plenty!"

"Oh, no," Lohe replied. "I have many children at home and my wife's mother will come, too." He kept on walking.

"Just one fish," the woman begged. "I'm so hungry."

"I've just enough for my family," Lohe said, a little angry and a little frightened, too. "Look, the ʻāweoweo are running today. Just go down to the shore and you can catch all you can eat, just like I did."

Lohe picked up speed to get away from the old woman. When the path turned, he looked back but he could not see her. She must have gone down toward Kōloa, he decided happily; at least she wasn't following him.

He hurried along. The sun was hot on his skin and the air around him got hotter and hotter and sweat seeped from every pore. The road seemed much longer and wound about in a very confusing way. Soon he was so hot and tired all he could do was place one foot before the other, first the right foot, then the left foot, each footstep causing a puff of hot dry dust to rise up to his mouth and nose, making him long for a drink of water. He was so thirsty that his tongue stuck to the roof of his mouth. At last he reached the top of the rise and turned toward his home. He heard a stream flowing over its bed and the tinkling of water had never sounded so delightful. He dropped his bundle of fish in the shade of a bush and flopped down in the shallow stream, letting the cool water flow over him as he drank his fill.

When he reluctantly got up from the water, he was pleased to feel the air had cooled considerably. It was not such a hot day after all! He took a deep breath of fresh air. He frowned, wrinkled his nose, and sniffed. What was that awful smell?

Lohe ran to his container of fish and flipped open the lid. Inside the gourd there were no longer fresh fish staring up at him with big eyes. There was only a liquid pool of rotting fish. A terrible smell rose from the gourd and surrounded him. He choked and felt sick, turned and ran all the way home, stopping along the way to scrub his skin in every stream he crossed, but the smell of rotten fish was still strong when he at last stopped outside his own door. His wife refused to let him come near her. "You stink," she said truthfully, holding her nose. "You are a terrible fisherman! I didn't eat a banana all day, but all you can bring home is the smell of rotten fish."

Just then his wife's mother Hina came by. She took a couple of delicate sniffs. "What happened to you?" she asked, wrinkling her nose at the awful smell.

Lohe told her of his day, of catching the fish, of the old woman under the kukui tree, of the heat of the sun, and of the gourd container suddenly full of rotten fish.

Hina nodded understandingly. "No wonder," she laughed. "Good for her! You should have given that old woman some fish before she even asked for it. That is our way, to share what we have. You could have given her a quarter of the fish, for you had plenty. A taste of fish with our poi would have been enough. Now we have no fish to eat at all."

"But how could the fish have become rotten so quickly?" wondered Lohe.

Hina replied, "The old woman was Pele, the goddess of fire. When you were so greedy and refused her request, she was angry. She made the air around you hot and she spoiled your catch of fish. Easy enough for her!"

"The next time an old woman asks me for something, I'll give it to her," Lohe promised.

Hina laughed. "Pele doesn't always appear as an old woman. There's no telling what form she'll take. You had just better learn to share what you have!"

The stream that Lohe drank from was named Weoweo-pilau, Stinking-weoweo fish, for the smell of rotten big-eyed fish lingered for a long, long time. Lohe's friends saw where his footsteps had criss-crossed the trail time and again and they named the nearby hill Ka-hoa-ea, Caused-to-wander. His friends never let him forget his adventure with the old woman under the kukui tree, and after that Lohe kept a sharp eye out for gray-haired women, and he was always careful to share what food he had with them.

Pīkoi a me Puapualenalena

"What can I learn from a dog?" Pīkoi protested. "I am Pīkoi, son of ʻAlalā, and the best shot on the island with my bow and arrow. No one can do better than I can."

The man sitting across the fire from him smiled and shook his head. "Aʻo," he said. "Learn."

The old man never spoke much for he was a stranger to the island of Kauaʻi. A few years before there had been a great storm. Huge swells had swept down from the north to dash angrily on the shores, shifting the sand from their summer beach to their winter home. One night those along the shores of Kapaʻa heard a sound they'd never heard before, a sharp "ʻaoa, ʻaoa" repeated over and over again.

A few brave men and women had dashed out and seen a strange sight. Coming in on the breakers was a canoe unlike any they'd seen before and in the canoe a man lay slumped over, arms dangling in the water. Dead, thought the people. Behind the man in the canoe was a dog. It was, they said later, bigger than any dog had a right to be and therefore must be related to Kūʻīlioloa, a god who could assume the form of man or dog at will. But the people did not have long to look, for a swell crested and broke, driving the canoe onto the rocks to be smashed to bits. The man was thrown into the water and the dog jumped after him, grabbed him by the collar of the strange clothing he was wearing and swam for shore.

Now that same man was telling Pīkoi he could learn from the dog.

Pīkoi was angry. Dogs were raised only for food. They were small with short tails and short ears and they were completely silent except for a growl or a little yip when someone stepped on them. Pīkoi looked across the fire at the dog that had come ashore from some far land across the ocean. This dog had long hair of blue-gray and white, sharp pointed ears, and a tail of brownish yellow hair that streamed in the wind like the feathers of a flying rooster. Because of that tail, everyone called the dog Puapualenalena, Yellow tail feathers. Even odder, the dog had one blue eye and one green eye. As he looked, it seemed to Pīkoi that Puapualenalena closed his green eye to stare at him with his blue eye and grinned. The dog's long pink tongue stuck out like a warrior's before battle — in an attempt to insult one's enemy and get his anger up.

Pīkoi was angry. "All right," he said. "We'll go out hunting tomorrow. We'll see who catches the most rats!"

The old man said, "No, no contest. Show. You show him, he show you."

Pīkoi's anger turned to curiosity. He was a very skillful boy, very clear and farsighted. He had already surpassed all the men of Kaua'i in his ability to kill hidden and far-off rats. In fact, he was now welcoming the challenge. He liked learning new skills. He did not know what a dog could teach him, but he would go.

The morning was clear and sunny, a perfect day for sighting rats. Pīkoi and Puapualenalena rambled up the banks of Wailua River and began climbing the hill of 'A'āhoaka. Near the top of the hill there was a little nest of rats. Pīkoi could see two rats peering down at them, their noses quivering, deciding whether to hide or run. Swiftly Pīkoi armed his bow with an arrow but his foot stepped on a twig which snapped loudly. The rats disappeared and Pīkoi could not see where they were.

Puapualenalena arched his feet high, one by one, as he maneuvered across the ground, carefully placing one foot down, then the other. Pīkoi realized the dog made no sound as it moved along warily, heading for the two rats which once again were foolishly peering out around the blades of grass they thought were hiding them. Puapualenalena pounced and the rats were no more.

The two continued to walk along, but Puapualenalena, it seemed, was more aware of rats than the boy was. Pīkoi watched in amazement as the dog brought him rat after rat he had not seen or that his clumsy way of moving had frightened into hiding.

Suddenly Puapualenalena stopped, his green and blue eyes peering intently ahead, his body quivering.

"What is it?" Pīkoi asked.

The dog could not answer of course, but he suddenly bounded forward. Pīkoi heard the click of teeth clamping together and Puapualenalena returned bearing a small gray rat in his mouth. He laid the rat at Pīkoi's feet.

"I did not see that," Pīkoi said. "Now I'll find one before you do."

A boy and a dog hunt together

Pīkoi set off up the hill, carefully searching every rock that might hide a rat, every rustling blade of grass that might betray that rat's movement. In a certain angle of the sun he saw a glitter, and carefully notching his sugar cane tassel arrow tipped with kauila wood, he pulled his bow and loosed the arrow. Pīkoi heard the thump of the arrow striking home and a faint squeal and shouted with joy. He ran forward to pick up his rat, neatly impaled through the eye and went to show it to Puapualenalena.

"Now we're even," Pīkoi said.

But soon Puapualenalena moved aside and Pikoi saw that the dog now had two rats. When had he caught the second one? Pīkoi wondered. Suddenly Pīkoi understood what the old man of the ocean had meant. He could learn from a dog, from such a dog as Puapualenalena.

"I can shoot six rats with my ten arrows," Pīkoi said, "and that's still better than most men on Kaua'i. I can kill a rat as far away as I can see one, but I don't always see them."

Pīkoi held his hand out to the dog and Puapualenalena moved in close until the hand brushed the coat of hair. It was softer than anything Pīkoi had ever felt before and he was pleased for the dog had never allowed anyone but his master to touch him before.

"Yes," Pīkoi said, "I certainly can learn from you, Puapualenalena."

They continued up the river, past Pu'upilo, past the waterfall of Koholālele. Here Pīkoi saw the rats first and this time he got three. Puapualenalena also caught three. They rambled the plains between Hanahanapuni and Mauna'ou, and hunted the stream banks of Waikoko, Waiahi, and 'Ili'ili'ula.

As the days flew past, the boy grew taller and stronger and his eyes were keener than ever before. The dog taught him well how to observe, how to look for the faintest trace of a rat, for the mere whisper of a whisker not hidden, the merest flash of a glittering eye, the faint difference between a tail being whisked out of sight or an earthworm's movement.

The dog moved silently. He never growled or whined, yelped or yipped, and never barked. His green eye and his blue eye, his lolling tongue and cheerful smile never allowed Pīkoi to appear foolish. Pīkoi untangled the plumes of Puapualenalena's tail and pulled out the burrs and brushed his coat. The two became inseparable friends.

One night, when dog and boy were seated across the fire from the old man from the outer seas, the old man said, "Tomorrow, contest."

Pīkoi stayed up late checking over each of his arrow shafts. These were made of sugar cane flower stalks that had been soaked in mud and allowed to dry. Each shaft was tipped with a sliver of hard, dark red kauila wood to give a killing edge to the dart. Pīkoi checked his bow of wauke wood and wove a new two-ply cord of hau bark and looped it over the ends of the bow. When he was sure his equipment was ready, Pīkoi lay down to sleep.

Puapualenalena flopped down beside him with a sigh, put his head on his paws and looked at the boy with his one green eye and his one blue one. Then the eyes closed and boy and dog slept.

It was the not the best of days to hunt. It was overcast and the light was flat and there were no shadows. The two roamed over the plains between Nounou Range and Kamanu Ridge, between the banks of the south and north branches of the Wailua River. Both moved carefully, searching near, searching far for the slightest trace of a rat. They stayed near each other. They wandered apart. By noon Puapualenalena had four rats to Pīkoi's two. When the sun was setting behind the mountain ridges, boy and dog returned to the fire and showed the old man from the outer ocean their catch. Each had killed ten rats. The contest was even.

"Good," the old man said. "Tomorrow, contest."

This second day was a hunter's dream. Bright sunshine flooded the land, making bold shadows. Even the shaking antennae of grasshoppers were easily seen. Once again boy and dog roamed the plains, searching for each and every rat that was there. Never had there been such hunting! The rats could not even breathe inside their nests before an arrow found them or the snapping of large white teeth through their necks was the last thing they heard. They moved silently, the boy and the dog, for the boy had learned well. Pīkoi felt the sun on his skin, felt the breeze in his hair, felt the solid ground under his feet, and felt the companionship of Puapualenalena and was happy. But he had no intention of letting the dog beat him! He searched and watched and collected forty rats.

Puapualenalena had also collected forty rats, a tie in the contest. The old man chuckled. "You have learned well."

And then Puapualenalena grinned and looked at Pīkoi with one green eye and one blue eye, and barked, "'Aoa, 'aoa!"

'Ualaka'a

One evening after farmers had returned to their thatched houses by the sea and the wind breathed softly through the leaves, Rat and Rooster spoke to one another. They had been chased from Kapānaiʻa's kula land, dodging the stones the farmer had thrown, and had eaten their fill in the fields of Kūpihe.

Rat said, "It would be hard to find food if all farmers were like Kapānaiʻa."

Rooster replied, "Indeed, we must be thankful for Kūpihe." He watched as his chicks and his hens foraged one last time in Kūpihe's field before going to their tree to roost for the night.

"Such hospitality should be repaid," Rat said.

"I have long thought the same," Rooster said, "but I do not know how."

"We must study the matter," Rat said. "We will find a way."

"Yes, we must watch for our chance," Rooster said. "Who knows, perhaps there is really something we can do." Rooster was grateful but, having a chicken's brain, he did not have much room for thought.

Rat, however, had a rat's brain. It was agile and clever and Rat knew he would find a way.

Kūpihe and Kapānaiʻa were two farmers who lived near the Waimea River mouth in thatched houses. Kapānaiʻa's house was surrounded by a solid stone fence with very even square corners. Kūpihe's fence was of driftwood collected from the beach and was not at all tidy to look at. They each had a piece of farming land for growing those crops that did not need constant water. Kapānaiʻa's field was built up on a platform on a ridge. Kūpihe's field was down on the flats below that of Kapānaiʻa and it seemed more a jungle of plants than a farm.

The two men were not friends. When they walked from their houses to their fields, they did not go together. Indeed Kūpihe was everything Kapānaiʻa did not like.

Kapānaiʻa was a practical, provident farmer. He observed every prayer, every ritual he had ever heard of for the success of his farming. Each tiny parcel was planted at the right moment, a little now, a little later on, and so Kapānaiʻa had food for his family all year long. He believed that food should be planted during the suitable months and that food was a child to be cared for. It was a heavy responsibility. He was keenly aware of the need to give food to his landlord, the konohiki of Waimea. Each day Kapānaiʻa inspected each orderly plant for insects. Caterpillars were immediately crushed between rocks. He threw stones at any bird that dared to pass overhead, and his special hate was the wild chickens. Roosters, their hens and their chicks, loved insects and seeds and did not care that Kapānaiʻa claimed all within his field. He threw stones at them and the chickens learned to come only in the early morning and late evening. Kapānaiʻa made traps but found that wild chickens make tough eating. Rats he hated most of all, for they nibbled on the ripening gourds and yams and sweet potatoes and spoiled the fruit.

Kūpihe, on the other hand, was a dreamer and an improvident farmer. He planted everything at the same time. Everything grew and everything ripened at the same time, and to keep from wasting anything, Kūpihe would invite his neighbors to a feast. Kapānaiʻa, of course, never came. Kūpihe was filled with awe over the beauty of the land and ocean and sky around him. Passing clouds drew pictures of wonder for him. The pounding surf gave him a cadence that he would turn into the rhythm of a dance. Kūpihe loved to chant, sing, and dance. He would pray to all the gods, calling them by name, especially to Kānepuaʻa, god of agriculture. Whenever the konohiki demanded food as was his right, Kūpihe would be surprised and wave his hand in the general direction of his fields and tell the konohiki to help himself to whatever there was. He paid little attention to the insects, birds, chickens, or rats. If he did, he was just as apt to study them with affection and turn their motions into a dance. He was famous for his chicken dance and his rat dance. His field grew wild and there was plenty of food for him and the chickens and the rats.

One day, the konohiki announced that the ruling chief was offering a prize to the farmer who could grow the largest, most perfect sweet potato. It had to be large and excellent eating however prepared. All farmers were ordered to participate. The winner would receive his choice of new taro fields and he who did not try would lose his land.

Kūpihe shrugged and went to his field and dug a hole and placed three starts of mōhihi ʻuala, which was quick growing and sometimes got quite big. He watered it, told it what was expected, and forgot all about it. The mōhihi, naturally, did its best but could not compete with all the riot of growth about it and the ravages of cutworms and weevils and grew only to modest size.

Kapānai‘a was determined to win the prize. He went to his field and burned off all the grass and shrubs and dug over the soil thoroughly after a good shower had softened the ground. He fertilized it with rotted leaves. In the early morning, as was proper, he planted three slips to each mound and watered them. Day after day he weeded, dug out the small potatoes with his fingers, and left only one potato in the hillock to grow and grow and grow. Soon it was huge and part of it grew above ground, in the center of purple stem vines, with dark green leaves and pinkish lavender flowers. Kapānai‘a was certain he would win the prize.

That night the moon rose silently and smiled on the land below. The stars glittered brightly and the unruffled surface of the river reflected the upside-down images of the houses and trees along its bank. Rat went into Kapānai‘a's field and looked at the ‘uala. Then he walked slowly down to Kūpihe's field and searched the overgrown fields. At last he found what he wanted, a small place where no food plants grew.

Rat went to Rooster's tree. "Rooster," he called.

Sleepily, Rooster answered. "Ēō! What do you want?"

"Come, we must go to work," Rat said.

The stars were bright, the moon brighter still, and the two went to Kūpihe's field. "We must dig up the ground here," Rat said, showing Rooster the place. Rooster scratched with his feet, sending up a shower of dirt while Rat clawed away until a goodly hole appeared.

"Now what?" Rooster asked, yawning.

"Now we move an ‘uala," Rat said and led the way to Kapānai‘a's field. Carefully the two of them scratched the earth away from the tuber and Rat bit the vine, freeing the tuber from his hillock. Slowly Rooster and Rat rolled the ‘uala tuber down the hill and into the prepared spot in Kūpihe's field. Then the two returned to rest.

At dawn Kapānai‘a, who had hardly slept worrying about his huge ‘uala, rushed to his kula field. He went to his hillock but there was no lump in the hill hiding under the purple-stemmed vine. He felt into the pu‘e but there were no tubers at all. He looked here, he looked there, but he could not find his sweet potato. He stood at the edge of his platform and saw Kūpihe enter his own overgrown field. He heard Kūpihe call out in surprise and hurried down.

‘Ualaka‘a

He found Kūpihe piling up the soil around a hillock which held the largest sweet potato Kapānaiʻa had ever seen, one that looked, indeed, exactly like his.

Kapānaiʻa stood there until he was able to say, "Whose potato is this?"

Kūpihe said, "I suppose it is mine, for it is growing in my potato hill in my field."

Kapānaiʻa replied, "No, it is mine. Return it to me."

"How can I do that?" Kūpihe asked. "It is growing solidly here."

"Return it to me," Kapānaiʻa demanded angrily, "or I shall call the konohiki and he will make you return what is rightfully mine."

"But it is growing in my field," Kūpihe replied. "It is not growing in your field which is up there. Does a sweet potato walk?"

"Remain here," Kapānaiʻa ordered. He ran to fetch the konohiki.

Kūpihe shrugged. He had no reason to go elsewhere. True, he did not remember planting this particular sweet potato in this particular place. He saw four dark shining eyes staring at him from a patch of shrubs. He saw Rat and Rooster standing side by side. "Did you have something to do with this?" he asked.

Rooster crowed.

Rat squeaked.

Kūpihe grinned. "Thank you," he said.

Just then, Kapānaiʻa and the konohiki came. Kapānaiʻa showed him the ʻuala growing in Kūpihe's field, and claimed it as his own.

"Is it an ʻuala kaʻa," the konohiki asked, "that can travel from one field to another? How can that be? No, a sweet potato grows where it is planted and cannot move from field to field. Yours must have dried up during the night. Did you give it enough water?"

Kapānaiʻa could say nothing for he could not explain what had happened. His bitterness knew no end when Kūpihe won the contest and found others willing to work his wet-land fields while he composed new songs and dances for the entertainment of all.

Kūpihe continued to plant everything all at once, and sing and dance, and enjoy all the bounties he had been given: the peaceful river, the green banks, pleasant shade trees, coconut fronds dancing in the wind, birds flitting, chirping, and singing among them. Whenever he harvested, Kūpihe left an extra helping in the field for his friends, Rat and Rooster.

He Kaʻao no ka ʻŌhelo Kahi

CHRISTINE FAYÉ © 96

Each summer, the birdcatcher Maunakepa, his wife Hoʻoleiʻa, and their daughter Helohelo lived in the mountains beside the great swamps and lehua forests that stretch from Ka-unu-o-Hua to Waiʻaleʻale. Here Maunakepa built a solid house thatched with bulrushes.

Each day he would go into the forest and set traps for the red olokele and ʻapapane birds, the yellow ʻamakihi, and the yellow and black ʻōʻō. Some of these birds he trapped in breadfruit gum he had spread on the branches where they liked to sit and sing. Others he caught in small mesh nets strung between two trees. Maunakepa could whistle the call of any bird that lived in the mountains and could sit without moving for hours so that the birds mistook him for a stone.

Maunakepa pulled just a few feathers from each bird and let it fly free. Hoʻoleiʻa sewed the feathers into little bunches and put them carefully away in a large gourd container where they would be protected from the rain.

As a baby Helohelo watched her parents and as she grew older, she could imitate a bird's whistle so well that they came flocking around her. She learned how to remain so still, holding a lehua flower in her hand, that a honeycreeper would fly to it and feed from it. She could move so silently through the wood that no bird flew in fright. As she roamed through the woods, Helohelo left little offerings to Laka, the goddess of the forest, to Kūhuluhulu, god of the bird-catchers, and to many other gods and goddesses as well.

She was a sturdy, straight-backed child with cheeks that were flushed by good health. It was this rosiness, helohelo, that gave her her name.

But one day, she felt very tired and her bones ached and she spent the day lying quietly on her bed. By evening, a fever had begun.

"We must get some medicine from the kahuna lapaʻau, the doctor," Hoʻoleiʻa said.

"We have no way to pay him," Helohelo protested. "Don't worry, I'll be fine tomorrow." She said a prayer to Lonopūhā, the god of healing.

During the night, the fever grew hotter. Maunakepa agreed with his wife. Medicine they needed, medicine they would have, even though he had nothing to give for the medicine. The feathers belonged to the high chief, so did the birds in the forests. No matter, whatever the doctor asked for payment, he would get.

Before dawn, Maunakepa ran down the path to the village at Pu'ukāpele but there was no healing priest there. He ran down the ridge toward Mānā and along the way he came across a man dressed in a white kihei sitting under a tree. There were many calabashes in their traveling netting grouped around him.

"Where are you going so fast?" the man asked.

"I am looking for a kahuna lapa'au," Maunakepa said.

"And what for?" asked the man.

"My daughter has a fever and it grows hotter with every hour," Maunakepa said. "I must have medicine to heal her."

"What luck!" exclaimed the man. "I am a healing priest."

Maunakepa sighed with relief. "You know my errand," he said.

"Indeed," said the priest. "But what will you give to the god of healing and to me for the medicine you need?"

"I have nothing," Maunakepa said. "I will get what is required, however."

"Yes, well, we shall see," said the priest doubtfully. "There are many things I will need. First of all, I will need some alaea, the red dirt from Ka-lua-alaea. No other red dirt will do."

Maunakepa thought for a moment. Ka-lua-alaea was a small valley in the canyon. He would have to climb the ridge again, go down at Kukui and down the steep path. But once there he could dig the red dirt for himself and would not have to barter for it. "I can get that," Maunakepa said and started to go.

"Wait!" said the kahuna. "It will be good to have alaea, but I am not sure it is enough of an offering for the god of healing. You had better get some dark-backed shrimp from Kaluaokalani."

Kaluaokalani was a stream in the canyon not far from Ka-lua-alaea. Maunakepa could catch the shrimp by himself. "Yes," he said. "I can get that."

"One more thing," said the kahuna. "While you are about it, bring some 'awa from Kalua'ā. No offering to the gods is complete without 'awa."

A story of the first 'ōhelo plant

Maunakepa ran as fast as he could to get a handful of alaea, a dozen dark-backed shrimp, and some 'awa root. His heart was light, for before the day was over he knew he would have medicine that would cure Helohelo.

The priest waited where he was. It was too hot to wander around. His calabashes were full of fresh poi and salted fish he had gotten for treating patients in Mānā. He moved from place to place quickly before people discovered he really didn't know much about medicine. Since he really didn't believe in the gods, he always managed to forget to offer his portion to the god of healing, Lonopūhā.

It was late in the day before Maunakepa returned to the kahuna lapa'au with the things he had requested. The kahuna gave him a small gourd filled with some kind of liquid.

"Let your daughter drink of this," the kahuna said. "She will get better."

Maunakepa ran home and Ho'olei'a gave the medicine to Helohelo.

"Lonopūhā," Ho'olei'a prayed, "help my daughter to get well."

Through that night, Maunakepa and Ho'olei'a sat beside Helohelo while the fever grew hotter and hotter. The medicine had not helped. It only seemed to make things worse. Both parents offered up prayers and promises to Lonopūhā, god of healing. In the darkest part of the night, between midnight and dawn, Helohelo died in her parents' arms. Lonopūhā had failed to help them.

Unknown to them, Lonopūhā had heard from the great priest of Mānā that a priest had come to them, claiming in the name of the god to be able to heal the sick. But many of the ill had died. Now the head priest warned Lonopūhā that people were saying that he was a worthless god that would not help the sick recover.

Upset, Lonopūhā came to see for himself what was happening. He studied the sick, tasted the medicine they had been given, and knew it was worthless. Lonopūhā spent most of that day curing the sick of Mānā and it was not until late in the day that he could follow the footsteps of the false priest to where he sat under a koa tree, eating his poi flavored with salt mixed with alaea, the dark-backed shrimp, and drinking fresh 'awa.

Lonopūhā looked into the heart of the priest and saw only lies and deceit there. Angrily, the god turned the priest to stone, the death called make pa'u, stone-death. There he still sits beside the path although the koa tree is long gone.

He Ka'ao no ka 'Ōhelo Kahi

Then, in the morning, Lonopūhā went into the mountains to search for the sick child. He found the parents, weeping silently as they dug a grave for Helohelo. They lined it with palapalai fern and scattered red lehua blossoms in it. They laid Helohelo in the grave and covered it over and wept. Flocks of birds settled into the trees and sang a farewell.

Lonopūhā took great pity on the grieving parents, for they had done nothing wrong. He could not bring the dead back to life, but he would do what he could to make sure her memory never died.

Lonopūhā breathed gently over the grave of Helohelo. He eased the pain of Maunakepa and Hoʻoleiʻa and, in a dream, told them to watch over their daughter's grave.

A small shoot began to grow from the grave. Day by day, the shoot grew larger until it formed a shrub. This was a shrub no one had ever seen before. Then the shrub flowered and the flowers turned to a reddish-brown fruit the color of Helohelo's cheeks.

When the news of this strange plant reached the ears of the high chief, he came with all his retinue to see it for himself.

"What is the name of this bush?" the high chief demanded, but no one could tell him.

The high chief conferred with the gods and at last asked Lonopūhā.

"It shall be called ʻōhelo because its rosy color recalls the cheek of Helohelo," Lonopūhā told him.

When he heard this, the high chief said, "This bush shall be made kapu, forbidden to all. We shall name the land on my right hand Kapu-ka-ʻōhelo, Forbidden-is-the-ʻōhelo, and the land on my left hand Kapu-ka-lau-ʻōhelo, Forbidden-is-the-ʻōhelo-plant."

In the years that followed, the birds, who understood nothing of kapu, spread the berries here and there in the mountains and swamps. Many centuries later, Pele, before she became the goddess of the Hawaiian volcanoes, found these ʻōhelo berries and claimed them as her own and spread them to the other islands, but that is another story for another time.

A story of the first ʻōhelo plant

Ke Kahua o Mali'o

ekoa strode quickly along the Koaiʻe Stream, trying to escape the words of his parents still buzzing in his ears.

"It is time you married," his father had said.

He was not old enough, Kekoa had protested, and he had no home ready.

"It is time you married," his mother had said. Her words were a command. Kekoa knew that his parents were looking for a wife for him at that moment, but she might not be good to look upon.

He forded Hapalau Stream where it flowed into the Koaiʻe. Further up, he crossed over Ka-wai-iki and was not even aware his feet had gotten wet.

He came to Kalaʻaloa, where ferns grew that were gathered as an offering to Laka, the goddess of the hula. Here Kekoa picked three fronds and wove them into a circle. This lei he placed on a rock and said a prayer.

"Laka," he pleaded, "let my wife be someone who will delight my heart all my life."

Still caught in his gray misty thoughts, Kekoa continued up the valley. His foot slipped on a moss-covered boulder and he fell into the pond that lies at the foot of the Komaliu Waterfall. He emerged blowing and puffing.

Laughter echoed from the surrounding rocks.

Kekoa looked around, ready to attack. But instead of someone he could fight, there was a young woman staring at him from a rock beside the waterfall, her mouth wide with laughter. Her dress was of the finest kapa barkcloth of a color only the chiefs could wear. Her hair hung to her waist, she was without blemish, and Kekoa knew he wanted her as his wife.

Her laugh was pleasant and his blush of shame faded and he, too, began to laugh at the sheer pleasure of her.

"Will you marry me?" he asked, when he could.

She stopped laughing. "I can't," she replied.

"Why?" Kekoa asked. "Whose choice is it?"

But she shook her head. She could say no more. She smiled at Kekoa. "My name is Maliʻo," she said and walked under the waterfall and away.

Kekoa sat dreaming in the stream for a long time. He whispered, "Maliʻo!" Maliʻo is the first dawn of morning light and he knew that she would be the source of all light and comfort in his life, just as dawn promises the life-giving sun. Maliʻo would be his wife, but if she could not tell him how to win her, who could he ask? Kekoa smiled as he remembered Pueo, his foster father.

Pueo had cared for him when he was a baby. Pueo had rocked him on one foot and carried him on his shoulders. He knew many things, for he was a kahuna kilo, a priest who could see past and future. Kekoa ran to the home of Pueo.

Pueo sat his foster son in the shade of a tree and sat across the mat stroking his long white beard. Pueo's hair was white, his clothing was white, but there were spots of brown here and there, and these, with his hooked nose, made him resemble the bird whose name he bore. "What brings you here so out of breath?" Pueo asked.

"I have seen a beautiful woman named Maliʻo," Kekoa said. "My parents have said I must marry and I will marry only Maliʻo. Maliʻo is …," and his voice faded away as he remembered Maliʻo sitting on the rock laughing at him.

Pueo smiled. "Ho ohihi ka manaʻo i ka nani o Maliʻo, the mind is entranced with the beauty of Maliʻo, so marry her," he said. "No one has higher chiefly status than she. She has been set aside from birth for the man who will become her husband."

"I asked," Kekoa said, "but she said the choice wasn't hers."

"True," Pueo replied. "It is your choice, not hers."

"My choice?" Kekoa said. "But I have chosen." The look in Pueo's eye warned him.

"How can I win her?"

"You must capture her," Pueo said.

"That's easy!" Kekoa boasted with a grin of confidence.

"Try it," Pueo suggested.

In the next days, Kekoa tried. He swam across the pond and tried to follow her into the cave behind the waterfall, but rocks began to fall and he dared not go forward. He hid behind a boulder and tried to catch her unawares as she came through the cascade but she easily slipped from his grasp. He tried every trick he could think up with no success. After each attempt, Mali'o laughed but did not say a word. Kekoa returned to his foster father.

"It won't work," he said. "Please tell me what to do."

"First, you will need a canoe just big enough to sit in."

Kekoa asked the canoe makers to make him such a canoe. When it was done, he carried it back down to Pueo.

"Now you must gather all the cobwebs you can find," Pueo said.

Kekoa gathered cobwebs, catching them on broad taro leaves so they would not be broken. Day after day he gathered cobwebs until Pueo said, "Enough! Now, take the webs apart, leaving a long thread."

"Now, weave a three-strand cord," Pueo said. Kekoa wove the cord.

When the cord was done, Pueo said, "Now weave it into a net," and Kekoa wove a round net with a small mesh.

"You will never catch Mali'o," Pueo told his foster son. "She must come to you. You must sit in this canoe. She will see you and in her curiosity will come to the edge of the canoe. Then throw the net over her and she will become your wife. Be warned, you must not move, for she will not come to you unless she thinks you are an image. Now eat and rest."

Kekoa ate and slept and in the middle of the night Pueo woke him. Together they carried the canoe to the pond below the waterfall where Mali'o lived. Before Kekoa entered the canoe, Pueo said, "You must not move at all, even to blink your eyes. Otherwise, Mali'o will never come to you. Remember, do not move."

"Thank you," Kekoa said and hugged his kahu. Then he sat in the canoe and remained as still and silent as the stones themselves.

At dawn, Mali'o came out and stared in wonderment at the canoe floating in her pond, at the man, or perhaps an image, for it did not move, in the canoe. All day she watched and nothing moved. Night came and Mali'o peered out several times. Early in the morning, she dove into the pond and swam to the canoe to look more closely at this strange object.

At that moment, Kekoa threw his net at Mali'o and it settled down over her head.

She had caused Kekoa to become enraptured with her, ho'ohihi, and now he entangled her, hihi, with his love.

Very soon Pueo threw the black kapa of marriage over Kekoa and Maliʻo.

They lived beside the pond where they had met and it became known as Ke kahua o Maliʻo, the foundation of light and comfort, the source of Kekoa's happiness.

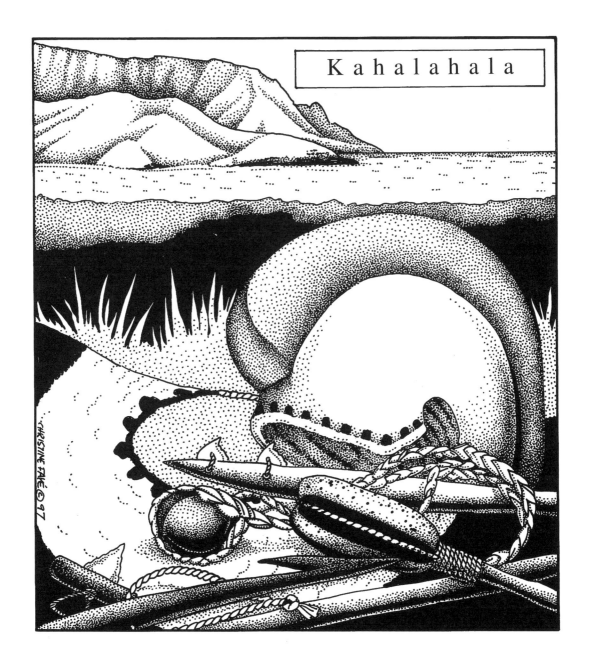

Chief Kauanohi examined the body lying on the beach. He did not like what he saw. "What do you think?" Kauanohi asked the kahuna lapaʻau, the expert in all medical knowledge, kneeling beside him. "Was he swept from the rocks of Makahoa?"

The doctor gently swept his fingers up and down the dead man's spine. "There is considerable bruising," he said, "such as might be caused by being dragged across rocks after death. See, here and here and here. Yet look at this bruise on his hip. He was still alive when he was struck there. That could be the first blow from falling on the rocks."

Kauanohi sensed the doubt in the doctor's voice. "But perhaps not?" he asked.

"Perhaps," the doctor said. "It is a peculiarly shaped bruise. Then look at his neck. It has been broken."

"Not by the waves," said Kihei, the chief's ilāmuku, the constable whose duties included the safety of the traveler on the road.

The kahuna lapaʻau shrugged. "It's possible that this was done by someone who knows lua." Lua was a form of hand-to-hand fighting that took years to learn. Its aim was to dislocate joints or break bones.

"Are you sure?" asked Kauanohi.

"No," admitted the doctor. "It's only a guess. But I think this man was dead when he went into the sea. Let us see." He grasped the cadaver by his waist and lifted the body up. He looked intently at the face of the dead man. "He was dead before he went into the sea. Look, there is no water flowing from his mouth."

Kauanohi glanced about the bay and the steep hillside that surrounded it. Too many bodies had been found on this particular stretch of beach in the lands of Waikoko. Usually a dead body here was due to an accident. Many travelers and peddlers preferred to skirt the headland of Makahoa, thinking the black lava leaf bordering the sea easier walking than following the trail over the headland and down again to the beach. Unexpectedly a sudden rogue wave could surge

Kahalahala ⚔

across the lava tongue and sweep away any human found there. Sometimes the ocean currents would bring the body ashore at this beach.

Once, twice a year, perhaps, a body would be found. That was sad but understandable. Then bodies had begun to appear until the sheer number of them over a short time began to cause wonder and then fear. Travelers and peddlers began to avoid this stretch of the road, and soon complaints came from Wainiha on one side and Hanalei on the other that the lack of supplies in and out of their lands was being felt. There was grumbling that the haku ʻāina, their landlord, was not doing his duty.

Since Kauanohi was the haku ʻāina, the chief in charge of the well-being of the district of Haleleʻa, it was his responsibility to discover what was happening. Now he, the kahuna lapaʻau, and the ilāmuku were on the beach between Makahoa Point and Hoʻohila's headland, the stretch of road known as Kealahula, carefully investigating the latest body.

Eyes were watching, Kauanohi was sure. He could sense them somewhere above him. "Ah, well," he said loudly, "another foolish traveler swept from the rocks of Makahoa. Bury him. Let us return; there is nothing to interest us here."

The doctor and the constable glanced quickly at each other. Kauanohi did not usually speak so loudly. Kihei ordered his men to dig a hole in the sand dunes and they carefully tied up the body in a sitting position so that he might greet his ancestors with dignity. Then the sand covered the stranger and Kauanohi led his men back to their headquarters in the valley of Wainiha.

Kauanohi said to his constable: "This must be the work of a kīmopō, a night robber. Send a man to spy on that valley day and night. He must hide up the ridge where he cannot be seen but can see well. Report back to me everything he sees."

Constable Kihei chose himself to become the sentinel. If the outlaw killing unwary and innocent travelers was a master of lua, who better to send than another such master? Like all lua-trained men, Kihei had large muscular shoulders and arms as strong as the branches of kauila trees. He too had plucked all the hair from his head and body and carefully oiled his body daily to keep his skin so slick no one could catch hold of him in a fight. Kihei had worked hard to master his art. If this kīmopō was using lua to kill and rob, it brought shame to all others who practiced lua. Such a man could not go unchallenged.

Kihei climbed the ridge that divides Lumahai from Waikoko, slowly working his way until he could command a view of the bay. Beneath a naupaka shrub he settled down and waited. For a long time he studied the land. He memorized each shrub, each tree, each leaf so that he would know of any disturbance. He listened to the sea, hissing and muttering as it spattered against the rocks and foamed onto the sand. The wind blew gently through the leaves, rustling dried hala leaves, soughing through the kukui trees, crackling the stems of the naupaka. An 'ūlili, a lone wandering tattler, called from the rocks where it searched for crabs and a kōlea, a golden plover, replied. He heard a rat nibbling in the grass. These were the sounds that were always here, the sounds of nature, and Kihei stopped listening to them.

It was mid-afternoon and Kihei's eyes were drooping with sleep when he heard voices coming from the Waikoko side. Whoever was singing was coming along the path over the ridge of Makahoa.

Below Kihei another voice softly called out: "Pihapiha, Kai o Kealahula, piha lele 'ū. The sea of Kealahula is rising and dashing high."

The voice was just below Kihei, a man's voice, calling quietly. Kihei realized that the man was against a small flat cliff that projected the voice well. Everyone in the little valley would be able to hear it, but not the travelers coming, making too much noise of their own to hear anything else.

Shortly a group of travelers came into view. Kihei watched as they continued along the path and went out of sight. The valley fell silent again.

At dusk Kihei watched as three men stepped from the trees below him and ran across the beach. Stripping off their malo of ti leaves, they plunged into the sea. They swam and scrubbed their skins with sand and Kihei noted that they made no noise. Three young men swimming together should make a lot of noise, with shouts and yelps as they ducked one another under the waves or splashed water into eyes, but these did not.

The first to emerge from the sea was a tall, broad man. His body was completely hairless; the hair on the head, his eyebrows, beard, and body hair had been pulled out. Kihei nodded to himself. This was a man skilled in the art of lua for only they showed such strength in the upper body and arms and pulled out all their hair. Such men were feared for they knew all the ways another man's body could be held and his bones broken. Usually these men were attached to a chief's court like Kihei himself and treated well. Why was this one by himself, not attached to a court? Kihei wondered. For there was no question in Kihei's mind. The man, now knotting his ti leaf malo in the tight fashion called pūʻali so that there would be little an adversary could catch hold of, was an ʻōlohe, a renegade, a robber, and as dangerous as any man-eating shark in the sea.

The other two men, Kihei decided, were simply servants to the ʻōlohe, for they were much smaller, carried no more than normal musculature, and their very movements as they hurriedly tied on their malo and followed the ʻōlohe back into whatever passed as their home announced their lesser role.

Kihei slipped away and reported back to his chief. "We need to know more," Kauanohi said. "Return tomorrow and watch."

By the last gleams of the setting moon, Kihei took up his watch under the naupaka bush. The dew was hardly dry when a lone traveler topped the ridge hurrying, obviously hoping to get through the valley quickly and unseen. Across his shoulder he carried a pole and from each end of the pole dangled large nets holding covered calabashes. From the way the pole sagged, the calabashes were heavy.

Once again a voice softly called out: "Malolo kai e! Malolo kai! The tide is low, low tide!"

As the traveler reached half way down the path to Kealahula, the large ʻōlohe stepped in front of him. The traveler turned to run, but the ʻōlohe caught him by the neck and swung him high off the ground, catching him by one hip. Kihei heard the snap of bones as the traveler went limp.

The ʻōlohe laughed. "Caught by Ka-puaʻa-pilau!" he gloated. "Caught by the lua fighter of Oʻahu! Never again shall a Kauaʻi man laugh at my name! You are killed by Ka-puaʻa-pilau!"

The ʻōlohe carried the traveler's body and dropped it into a large hole in the rocks at the foot of Makahoa headland. Then he returned, picked up the calabashes, and returned to his carefully concealed house under the trees.

Kihei returned immediately to Wainiha to report. He barely had time to rub kukui oil onto himself until his skin gleamed in the sun before he found himself leading a band of warriors back to Waikoko. They surrounded the hill and small valley and soon Ka-puaʻa-pilau and his two companions were flushed from cover. The two smaller men were quickly captured and tied hand and foot. None of Kihei's warriors dared get within reach of the 'ōlohe. To do so was to die. They formed a circle around him, each man holding a long spear and a short spear, their sharp tips pointing into the softest parts of the robber's body.

Ka-pua'a-pilau spotted Kihei. "I challenge you to single combat," he said.

"Indeed?" replied Kihei. "I deny your challenge."

"Perhaps you are a coward," Ka -pua'a-pilau said. "You are afraid to fight me." Ka-pua'a -pilau was hoping to get his opponent angry enough to fight. An angry opponent, he knew, was easier to defeat, for anger covered over clear thinking.

Kihei replied: "To fight you would be to dishonor me. You are a robber, a real stinking pig, pua'a pilau!"

It was the 'ōlohe who lost his temper at the insult to his name. With a roar, he rushed forward to grapple with Kihei. Ka-pua'a-pilau's hands slipped on Kihei's oily skin, but Kihei had no such problem for the robber's skin was dry. Kihei caught Ka-pua'a-pilau around the neck with one hand and under one knee with the other. He raised the robber above his head and brought him down hard across his knee, snapping the spine loudly. There was no honor in the death; it took only one blow, insult indeed.

Kihei ordered the body of Ka-pua'a-pilau thrown into the same hole he had thrown his victims into. As an afterthought, he ordered the other two robbers thrown in too.

In a few days, four bodies washed up onto the beach, the last unlucky traveler, Ka-pua'a-pilau, and his two companions.

Travelers once again freely walked the road between Waikoko and Wainiha. Yet no matter how carefree they seemed, they always hurried across the beach which they now called Kahalahala, the beach of dead bodies.

Who knew when another 'ōlohe might hide in this lonely place?

Pua and Hulu sat in their kapa house on top of the sand dunes of Kēʻē at Hāʻena. On one side of them breakers crashed onto the reef and rolled up on the sand. On the other side were the taro fields and fish ponds fed by Limahuli Stream, and beyond that, at the foot of the towering cliffs, was a deep cave filled with water. This water was fresh and clear and disappeared into the tunnel at the back of the cavern. Pua and Hulu did not know how deep that cave was, nor did anyone else, except maybe the moʻo maiden, Palai.

Day after day Pua and Hulu, who were sisters and lived with their husbands and children side by side, met at their kapa shed. They took the water-soaked strips of wauke bark from the taro patch and beat them into kapa to make clothing and bed coverings for their family. Each had anvils of deep red kauila wood but they were of different sizes, so Pua's anvil had a deep sound and Hulu's had a lighter, clearer sound. These two knew the secret of the beaters' code and could drum the latest news from the hula school at Kēʻē, and they knew that these would be passed on from anvil to anvil until everyone in the whole district of Haleleʻa, as far away as Kalihiwai, heard the gossip.

Of course, the latest gossip concerning Palai was eagerly awaited by their neighbors. Palai was a moʻo, part woman, part reptile, and naturally could live in the air and under the water. Every day Palai would emerge from the tunnel in the cave, swim to the edge, and climb up onto a ledge where her feet could dangle into the water. From this point, she could see out over the countryside and no one could approach her unseen. She would seat herself comfortably, nod at Hulu and Pua across the taro fields, and begin to comb her hair.

Palai had beautiful hair. It was brown and very long, reaching to her knees. Sometimes she brushed her hair forward, hiding her face and body. Sometimes she brushed her hair backward and the hair was a veil against which her lovely face and body were well outlined.

"Auwē, there must be a man coming," Hulu said when she saw Palai one day combing her hair backwards.

"Aren't they always?" laughed Pua.

The news they beat out on their anvils almost always concerned some young chief, attracted by Palai's beauty, who came to try his luck with her. Each chief would swagger up and down the entrance of the cave and talk brilliantly of his rank, or his parentage, or his genealogy back into the dim time of long ago. He talked of his wealth. He played some game or another with his friends to display the strength and prowess of his body. All in all, they provided much amusement and entertainment for the two women sitting on their sand dune across the way.

So far Palai had sent them all away but not until they had somehow or another made complete fools of themselves. Then Palai would dive into her pond and swim away out of sight and not come forth for several days while her lovesick youth hung around the entrance before finally giving up.

"I don't know what men see in her," said Hulu.

"She is beautiful," replied Pua.

"She is also a moʻo," replied Hulu. "And we know what that means."

"She is beautiful, she is capricious, she is dangerous, she is no one to be crossed, she can live in two worlds. A moʻo," agreed Pua.

"Exactly," Hulu said, giving a solid thunk to her anvil. "These young men would do better playing with fire. They'd be more apt to recover from their injury."

One fine morning, Hulu and Pua heard the noise of their neighbor's kapa anvil. "Kahakaloa, chief of Wainiha, is coming to Hāʻena to see the wonders of the watery cave for himself," the message read. Kahakaloa belonged to the ruling chief's family. He was wealthy, he was famed for his courage and for his physical beauty. Would Palai resist? Hulu and Pua were eager with anticipation.

It was already evening when Kahakaloa and his followers came walking slowly along the road. On the banks of the Limahuli Stream, they stopped to build a comfortable house for the chief to sleep in. Their spears were stacked up, the fishing nets spread out to dry, and kapa spread out for sleeping. A fire was built and freshly caught fish were grilled for their supper. They ignored the cluster of people, the families of Hulu and Pua, sitting on the sand dune watching everything they did.

In the morning, Hulu and Pua watched as Palai swam out of her cave and climbed onto her ledge and began to comb her hair.

"Backward," noted Hulu.

"Of course," said Pua, for the mo'o's hair, gleaming and blowing in the fresh morning trade wind, was a perfect background to display all her charms.

Kahakaloa approached and sat on a rock across the cave from Palai. He spoke quietly, Hulu and Pua noted, he did not make any kind of boast or try to show off. He merely sat, and Palai sat and the two talked throughout the morning. Then Palai stood up on her ledge, and stretched her arms over her head and dove into the water and disappeared.

That afternoon, the chief and many of his friends went to swim and fish in the ocean, while a work party, led by a man slightly older than the chief, approached the two women on their sand dune.

"We are looking for a place to dig an imu. Our lord is in no hurry to return home," said the luna of the work party.

Hulu and Pua laughed. He was not the first ali'i to be smitten with the charms of Palai. "Talk to our husbands," Hulu said. "They will show you where to dig an imu."

"You live here?" the man asked.

"Yes," Pua replied. "This is our home."

"Tell me about the mo'o," the man said. "I am Pahunui, companion and guardian of the young chief of Wainiha, Kahakaloa."

Pua indicated that Pahunui should sit. "Her name is Palai," she said. "She nods to us but we have never spoken so all we know is what we see and what we have heard about mo'o in general."

"Does she take many lovers?" Pahunui asked. "I know many men have come to court her."

"Never," Hulu said. "She always sends them away."

"Perhaps I am safe, then," Pahunui said. "She will send my chief away."

"Maybe not," Pua said. "She has never talked as long to one man before as she did your chief this morning."

"I hope he does not think she will make a wife for him," Hulu said. "A mo'o wouldn't be a very satisfactory wife, living in the water as well as on land. I think she would be as cold and unresponsive as a squid."

"And I don't think a mo'o would take very good care of children," Pua said.

"I have said all that and more," Pahunui said, shaking his head. "I don't think he is listening to me."

"Young men in love never listen to advice," Pua said.

"Easier to talk to the wind," Hulu added.

"True," Pahunui said. "But I will do what I can." With that, Pahunui left them to their work on the dunes and returned to care for his chief.

The following day, Kahakaloa and Palai again talked all morning, one on one side of the cave, his body, newly oiled with kukui oil, gleaming in the sun. Once again Palai dove into the water, her hair blowing out behind her and the chief returned to his friends.

The third day, the mo'o did not appear as usual at the entrance of her cave. The young chief also did not come out of his sleeping house. Pua and Hulu watched as Pahunui searched the camp. They saw him check the spears and the fishing gear, then run to the cave, searching here, searching there. He came running to the dunes.

"Have you seen my chief?" he asked.

"They are gone," Hulu said, "the chief and the mermaid are gone."

"Gone? Where?" Pahunui demanded.

"Into the cave," Pua said, "where Palai lives. She has never done this before."

"We must search for him," Pahunui said. "We will get canoes and go into the cave after them."

"Too late," said Hulu. "You will never find them. Just inside the tunnel, the cave branches into two. Which way will you go? Right? Left? Will your torches last in that darkness? Only the mo'o knows the secret of light within that cave."

"Let them alone," Pua said. "They will soon tire of one another and they'll come back of their own accord."

After several days, Pahunui led his troop back to Wainiha. Month after month went past. There was no sign of the mo'o and the chief.

The full moon shone in the sky ten times before Hulu and Pua looked over the taro fields to the cave and saw Palai sitting on her ledge, combing her hair with one hand. In her other hand she held a baby to her breast.

Bursting with curiosity, Hulu and Pua crossed the fields until they were close enough to talk to the mo'o.

Hulu said, "You have come back, have you?"

Palai nodded.

"And you have a baby at your breast," Pua said.

Palai nodded and smiled down at the infant.

"And where is the chief of Wainiha?" Hulu asked

Palai drew a finger across her throat. "Make i ka pahi! Dead by the knife!" she said and chuckled.

Hulu and Pua agreed later they had never been so frightened in their lives as they were at the sound of that chuckle.

The mo'o dove back into her pond and disappeared into the clear, clean water. Hulu and Pua hurried back to their anvils and beat out the message of Palai's return.

The next day, Pahunui and a great mob of furious people from Wainiha hurried to the cave armed with spears and clubs, sticks and stones, with any weapon that had come to hand. They stopped before the cave and waited for the mo'o to appear.

Palai did appear late in the morning, without the infant in her arms and without her comb. She stood on her ledge, her hair covering her from head to toe.

Pahunui, carrying his spear ready to throw, strode up to the edge of the lake. "Where is my prince?" he demanded.

Palai laughed and drew her finger across her throat.

Pahunui raised his spear and was just about to launch it when Palai said, with a sneering laugh, "Hoka! Hoka! Shame! Shame!"

She quickly dove into the water, her great masses of hair spreading out behind her, filling the lake from side to side, from the entrance into the tunnel at the back. Bubbles continued to rise from the pool, but although Pahunui waited, hour after hour, nothing more was to be seen of the mo'o.

Only the brown of Palai's hair staining the water remained. Never again did Hulu and Pua, beating kapa on their dune across the fields, see the mo'o of the cave that was ever after called Ka-wai-o-Palai, The-lake-of-Palai.

As the years went by and Hulu and Pua aged, the brown hair of Palai slowly turned gray, for the mo'o, too, was mortal and grew old. And she must have died, for the grayness of the water has disappeared and now the water is covered with scum and people toss cans and broken bottles into it and do not know that this is where Kahakaloa fell in love with a moʻo maiden and lost his life because of his love.

Nā Kia Manu a me Nā Moa Makanahele

Tūtū Nāhulu was the most skillful feather lei maker in all Kaua'i. Her two grandsons were excellent kia manu, birdcatchers, who collected the red, yellow, green, and black feathers that she tied into beautiful head and neck wreaths. Every high chief wanted to wear a feather lei made by Tūtū Nāhulu and traded food and clothing for them, so these birdcatchers always had plenty to eat and good clothes to wear.

One day, Tūtū Nāhulu and her grandsons went to collect feathers of nā moa makanahele, the wild forest chickens. They walked up the river bank to the tall green cliffs that climbed straight up to Mount Wai'ale'ale. There, at the foot of Kamanu peak, the boys built a house to shelter them from the rain. The oldest boy, who was as quick and darting as the forest birds, was named Wa'awa'a-iki-na'au-ao, and the younger boy, who was as slow and patient as the ocean birds, was named Wa'awa'a-iki-na'au-pō. As these names were too much alike and too hard to say easily, Tūtū Nāhulu called the older one Featherhead and the younger Birdbrain.

From the doorway of their new home Tūtū Nāhulu counted the waterfalls tumbling thousands of feet down the green cliffs and listened to the rumbling of the falling water. The river chattered to her as it swirled around the huge black boulders in the river bed. Far off, she heard the crowing of the wild forest chickens.

Tūtū Nāhulu loved to eat wild chickens. "Grandsons," she said, "please catch some chickens for me to eat."

The two birdcatchers, who always did whatever Tūtū Nāhulu asked them to do, went to catch some chickens. First they made an offering to Kū-huluhulu-manu, who was the god of all birdcatchers. Kū-huluhulu-manu was covered with black and red feathers and had large white staring eyes and a long beak lined with sharp teeth. A single yellow feather hung down over his forehead. If the god was pleased, the yellow feather would flutter and the two birdcatchers would catch many birds. If Kū-huluhulu-manu was angry, the boys knew they would catch nothing at all. This morning the yellow feather fluttered and the two boys set out happily to catch wild chickens for their grandmother.

After a while, Featherhead said to his younger brother Birdbrain, "You go that way to catch chickens and I'll go this way. We'll meet here at twilight. Then we'll make a pile of all the birds we catch and divide them up. Every chicken that has two holes in its beak will belong to me. Those that have one hole will be yours. The one of us who has fewer chickens must pluck the feathers and grill the birds over a fire."

Birdbrain agreed happily. He was glad to learn how to tell his brother's chickens from his own.

Soon Birdbrain saw a green grasshopper sitting on a blade of grass, singing its song as it waggled its long antennae back and forth. He reached for it but as soon as the grasshopper saw his hand, it stopped singing and looked as if it were going to fly away. Birdbrain held his hand very still until the insect forgot it was there. Then he scooped it up in his hand and popped it into a small gourd bottle that hung from his malo or loincloth. As he walked along he caught several more grasshoppers.

Birdbrain found a small grassy spot with some bushes around it. He took a long thin cord, tied a small loop at one end, ran the other end of the rope through this loop, and made a larger noose which he spread out on the ground in a circle. He tied a grasshopper to a stick which he pushed into the ground in the center of the circle. Birdbrain then took the other end of the rope with him and crawled under a bush to wait.

Birdbrain waited very patiently. The insects in the grass began to sing again and the little birds began to flit about in the trees. A chicken peered out from behind a bush, carefully watching the grasshopper that was sitting on a leaf scraping its back feet together. Then the chicken rushed over and caught the grasshopper in its beak. Just as it tilted up its head to swallow the insect, Birdbrain pulled his end of the rope and the noose closed quickly, catching the chicken by its legs.

This is how a birdcatcher snares wild chickens. That day Birdbrain caught six wild chickens.

As twilight approached, Featherhead and Birdbrain met at their appointed spot and divided all the chickens they had caught. Birdbrain had his six chickens but Featherhead had caught none at all. Yet whenever Birdbrain looked at a chicken, he saw it had two holes in its beak and handed it to his brother. "This is yours," he said. "It has two holes in the beak." All six chickens had two holes in its beak, so only Featherhead got to carry chickens back to his grandmother to eat.

Birdbrain had to pluck the feathers from all the chickens. He put the soft brown feathers into a covered bowl and the long red tail feathers into another bowl. He was very careful not to break a quill or split a feather. When all the chickens were plucked, he built a fire and roasted the birds, turning them often so they wouldn't burn. Tūtū Nāhulu and Featherhead enjoyed eating the wild chickens very much, but Birdbrain was so tired he just lay down and went to sleep.

A few days later, Tūtū Nāhulu wanted some more chickens to eat, so she sent her grandsons up into the hills. Only, this time Tūtū Nāhulu asked Birdbrain, "Why did Featherhead have all those chickens while you had none? Why did you have to clean and cook them all without help?"

"Featherhead told me that all the chickens with two holes in its beak belonged to him," Birdbrain told his grandmother. "We didn't catch any birds with only one hole. Maybe this time!"

Tūtū Nāhulu smiled fondly at Birdbrain. "Every chicken has two holes in its beak. Featherhead fooled you. Would you like to fool Featherhead this time?" she asked.

Birdbrain nodded his head eagerly and grinned as she whispered in his ear. She handed him two large gourd containers and asked, "Do you remember what to do?"

"Yes, Tūtū Nāhulu," he answered and followed his brother. Later, when Featherhead said, "All the chickens with two holes in their beaks belong to me, just like before," Birdbrain quickly agreed, "Oh, yes, they are yours." And he clucked like a hen and crowed like a rooster as he ran off to catch grasshoppers.

That afternoon, Birdbrain helped load all the chickens they had caught on his brother's back for, once again, all of the beaks had just two holes. Featherhead walked down the path whistling happily, for he knew that he wouldn't have to pluck feathers or grill chickens over a hot fire.

As soon as Featherhead was out of sight, Birdbrain opened the gourds his grandmother had given him. He took out a ball of sticky breadfruit gum and smeared himself from head to foot. Then he shook out the feathers that filled the other bowl and rolled himself in them until he was completely covered with soft brown feathers. He stuck some long black and red feathers in his hair and small white feathers around his eyes and more feathers around his mouth. In the center of his forehead he put one long yellow feather.

Birdbrain looked at his reflection in the river. He thought he looked like a very large rooster or like the image of Kū-huluhulu-manu, the god of the birdcatchers. Either way he looked like an angry forest spirit. Birdbrain flapped his arms and ran down the path after his brother, crowing as loudly as he could.

Featherhead heard something running up behind him, crowing like a rooster. "Birdbrain, you can't scare me!" he said and turned to laugh at his brother. But it wasn't Birdbrain he saw on the path! It was a giant chicken with a crest of red and black feathers, large eyes and a hungry, wide-open mouth. There were feathers all over the monster's body, even on its toes. It was waving its wings fiercely and Featherhead thought he had never seen anything more horrible in all his life.

"There he is! Kokō, kokō! There he is!" the feathery monster yelled, pointing right at Featherhead. "There is the chicken thief! I shall catch him and eat him!"

Featherhead was sure this was Kū-huluhulu-manu coming after him. He threw his bundle of chickens at the monster and ran home as fast as he could, never once looking behind him.

Birdbrain laughed and laughed. Tūtū Nāhulu's plan had worked very well. That night it was Featherhead's turn to cook their dinner. Birdbrain picked up the chickens and walked happily home, plucking feathers off himself and crowing like a rooster: "Kokō! Kokō!"

Ka Ho'okolokolo o 'Elepaio

The chief of Waimea fell ill and withdrew into his house on the beach. It was summer, the sun was strong, the wind died, and it grew very hot. The chief became thirsty and called for a drink of water from the cold mountain spring at the source of ʻElekeninui Stream. He refused all other water, only the cold water of ʻElekeninui would do.

So Piʻiwai, who was his steward, took the chief's water bottle, a beautifully decorated gourd. He tied a strip of red kapa around the neck of this water gourd to mark it as belonging to his chief and forbidden for anyone except Piʻiwai and his chief to touch. Piʻiwai climbed the mountain side, up the ridge of Hoea to Puʻukāpele, from Puʻukāpele to Puʻuhinahina, on past Halemanu to the meadow of Kanaloahuluhulu. He climbed over the small ridge into Waineki Valley. He did not notice that a bright-eyed brown and white bird was flitting from tree to tree beside him. Each time the bird lit on a branch, he cocked his tail. The ribbons of red kapa intrigued him. What was this thing the man carried that waved so brightly? Where was he going? What was he doing in the mountains? The bird wanted answers to his questions for this was ʻElepaio, and he was very curious about the doings of others.

Piʻiwai followed Waineki Stream to Kokeʻe Stream and from there he walked to Kapu-ka-lau-o-ka-ʻōhelo, the source of ʻElekeninui. The bird followed.

There Piʻiwai filled his bottle with fresh, cold water. He placed the water gourd carefully under a clump of ukiuki and returned to the spring to drink some water before returning to his chief far down at the mouth of the river.

ʻElepaio, as soon as the man's back was turned, flew down and lit on the water gourd and inspected it carefully. He tapped it with his beak. Auwē! it was soft and his beak went deep into the thing and as ʻElepaio drew back his head, water followed his beak and began to spurt out. ʻElepaio hopped along the gourd and pecked again. This was fun! The object was softer than the tree bark he pecked to find the grubs and insects that were his food, and certainly water did not flow out of tree trunks. ʻElepaio pecked again and another spurt of water flowed out.

Ka Hoʻokolokolo o ʻElepaio

The water slowed to a trickle and ʻElepaio pecked again but soon no more water came out. ʻElepaio was disappointed the game was over. He heard the man coming back and flew quickly into the lehua tree above and, cocking his tail, looked down.

Piʻiwai saw the bird flying away. He picked up the gourd. It was light. He shook it and found it was empty. The gourd was riddled with little holes. He immediately knew it was the work of mischievous ʻElepaio, for no other mountain bird pecks holes searching for food.

Looking about he saw ʻElepaio sitting on a branch nearby. He was very angry for he would have to retrace his footsteps to find another water gourd and he did not know how long that would take, and his chief lay ill waiting for this cool, life-reviving drink. Piʻiwai picked up a stone and threw it at the bird.

The stone hit the bird on the leg and flaked away a little of the skin. ʻElepaio immediately flew off. He landed on the hillside across the Kokeʻe Stream and watched the man as he trudged unhappily back over his trail. ʻElepaio grew angrier and angrier. How dare the man throw a rock? He needed to be punished. ʻElepaio was very indignant and flew off, grumbling to himself.

He flew to the open meadow of Kanaloahuluhulu. Here he found ʻAnianiau sipping from a lehua flower. He was a shy bird and his feathers were green above and bright yellow below. The birdcatchers, if they were looking up at him as he flew through the tree tops mistook him for the sun, and if they were looking down from a hilltop on the canopy of trees mistook him for a leaf.

"Ē, ʻAnianiau, ē!" called ʻElepaio. "Ē, ʻAnianiau, ē!"

"Iōē," replied ʻAnianiau. "What is it?"

"The man hit me with a stone!" ʻElepaio said indignantly. "We must punish him or he will hurt all of us!"

"Ps-sect!" ʻAnianiau piped his simple unslurred call note. He knew ʻElepaio rather well and went on, "And what was the cause for this man's action?"

"Look, the stone has hurt my leg," ʻElepaio said, showing ʻAnianiau his wound. "Just because I pecked a few holes in the man's water gourd doesn't mean I'm in the wrong. He must be punished."

"Perhaps we should have a conference of the birds," ʻAnianiau suggested. "You must ask Pueo." Pueo, as the largest of the birds living in the forest and the wisest, was the ruler of all the mountain birds.

"I shall find him," 'Elepaio said and flew away.

In Noe valley, he found Pueo, the owl, staring at a rat from a perch on a koa tree branch.

"Ē! Pueo ē," 'Elepaio called. "Ē! Pueo, ē!"

The rat scuttled away. Pueo turned his head and looked at 'Elepaio with his huge eyes. "Iōē, I am here. What is it?" he asked.

"The man has hit me with a stone!" 'Elepaio said indignantly. "We must have a conference of the birds and punish him!"

"Ah," said Pueo. He knew 'Elepaio rather well and went on. "Yes, perhaps we should have a gathering of the birds."

"I shall tell the others," 'Elepaio said and flew away.

One by one, 'Elepaio found the other birds. 'Elepaio flew to Pōhaku-waʻawaʻa and found 'Akialoa in the top of a koa tree. 'Akialoa had an extremely long bill and his feathers were olive brown in color, and his head was sprinkled with little brown dots.

"Ē, 'Akialoa, ē!" called 'Elepaio. "Ē, 'Akialoa, ē!"

"Iōē," replied 'Akialoa. "What is it?"

'Elepaio said, "We are having a conference of the birds."

"I shall be there," said 'Akialoa.

He flew to Ka-nahuna-o-Kamapuʻupuʻu, where the first dogs had gone wild in the mountains, and there he found Olokele. He was brilliant orange-red in color and had a long, deeply curved bill. His favorite food was honey from the tubular lobelia flowers. 'Elepaio explained and Olokele said, "I, too, will be there."

'Elepaio found 'Apapane of the deep crimson feathers and black wings at Puʻu-o-Kila. He found 'Ōʻōʻāʻā, she with glossy black feathers and four brilliant yellow plumes under each wing at Awaawapuhi, the valley dug out by the eel. He found 'Akekeʻe, with his short conical bill whose mandibles are twisted in opposite directions, at Kapu-ka-ʻōhelo. He found Nukupuʻu, whose lower bill was only half as long as his upper one, at Kumuwela. In the late afternoon, as the shadows covered the ground and the air grew sharp, the birds gathered for their conference at Puʻuhinahina.

Pueo, as the largest of the birds and the wisest, was the leader of the conference.

"Ē! 'Elepaio!" Pueo called.

"Iōē!" replied 'Elepaio.

"Tell us what happened," Pueo said.

'Elepaio said, "I saw a man coming along Waineki and followed him. At 'Elekeninui, he filled a container with water. The container had a red ribbon tied to it. I flew down and pecked at it and the water inside came out. Then the man threw a stone and hurt me. He must be punished!"

The birds whispered to one another. Puaiohi trilled, 'Ō'ō'ā'ā whistled, 'Akialoa softly trilled, 'Akikiki chipped, 'Apapane, whose voice was the most beautiful of all, gave a rolling call, three whistles, five chucks, and drew out a long last note until Mukupu'u pulled on a tail feather and 'Apapane ended his song with a faint squawk. All fell silent when Pueo cleared his throat.

"Where is the blame in this matter?" Pueo asked. "The man must return to Waimea and seek another gourd so he can bring water to his ailing chief. The chief may die without that water. Is the man wrong to be angry with 'Elepaio?"

The birds looked at 'Elepaio.

'Elepaio flicked his tail uneasily. "Perhaps not," he admitted. This was not going the way he had planned. He began to grow angry and bitter words formed silently in his throat. You of bitter rump feathers, he would say to 'Amakihi. You are a stench in the air, he'd say to Olokele. You ought to be roasted over the coals even though you'd pollute the gravy, he would shout at Pueo.

"Should 'Elepaio have pecked holes in the water gourd?" Pueo asked and all the birds looked again at 'Elepaio, who said nothing.

Pueo said, gently, "'Elepaio, who was to blame?"

'Elepaio hung his head and replied, "Mine is the fault for pecking the water gourd of the man."

"Hewa hā 'oe, your fault indeed," Pueo said. "Don't complain about your sore leg any more. You earned it. The conference is over."

'Elepaio is still very curious and will follow any traveler along the paths of the mountains. He will fly very close and stare with his bright dark eyes and flick his tail high above his back. He will call out "'e-le-pa-io, 'e-le-pa-io" to introduce himself. But he will never again peck holes in a water gourd.

Nā Kia Manu a me Nā Mai‘a

E ven though it was summer and the bird-catching season, Tūtū Nāhulu and her grandsons lingered at their home at Maunahina in Wainiha Valley. The two boys visited with their friends while they could, for bird hunting is a lonely business and they could talk to none but themselves for several months.

Tūtū Nāhulu was the most skillful feather lei maker in all Kaua'i. Her two grandsons were kia manu, birdcatchers who collected brilliantly colored feathers from little birds in the lehua forests of the high mountains. The older boy, who was quick and darting as the forest birds, was named Wa'awa'a-iki-na'au-ao and the younger boy, who was slow and patient as the ocean birds, was named Wa'awa'a-iki-na'au-pō. As these names were too much alike and hard to say easily, Tūtū Nāhulu called the older one Featherhead and the younger answered to Birdbrain.

One day, when evening shadows covered the valley, Featherhead came rushing home. "Tūtū Nāhulu!" he said excitedly. "Guess what? There is going to be a contest! The finest bunch of bananas will win the prize!"

"Ah," Tūtū Nāhulu said. "How I'd like a dish of pepeie'e, bananas and coconut cream wrapped in ti leaves and baked in the oven!" Her eyes gleamed as she thought of eating her favorite pudding.

Featherhead did not hear her. "I remember where there are some wonderful bunches of bananas. I know I can win this contest! I know it! Birdbrain will help me."

Birdbrain nodded. He would help and he would also see that Tūtū Nāhulu would have her pepeie'e.

The next morning, Featherhead rushed empty handed along the path up the valley, wanting to find the banana bunches he remembered before anyone else got to them.

Birdbrain trudged along quite far behind his brother. Before leaving home, he had seen that Tūtū Nāhulu had enough food on hand for the day. He had given some sugar cane to Kūhuluhulu,

Nā Kia Manu a me Nā Mai'a ✒

god of the birdcatchers, and chanted a brief prayer for the success of his brother in winning this contest. He also left a sacrifice and a prayer to Kūmauna, the god who lived in the mountains, for he was a banana planter as well as a rain god.

Then Birdbrain picked up his carved ʻauamo, a carrying stick of kauila wood. On each end he had carved a man's face and had whittled out notches so that whatever was hung on the ʻauamo with net bags would not slip off. Then he started out after his brother.

"All the bananas with yellow skins are mine," Featherhead told his brother. "All the rest with mixed colors are yours."

Birdbrain nodded. He was happy to know which bananas were his and which belonged to his brother.

They passed the village of Pōhakuloa and found a clump of maiʻa ʻeleʻele, a mountain banana with a black trunk. Dark green hands of fruit were already turning yellow. Featherhead knew that the fruit was good when cooked. Maybe this would win the prize. He grabbed the cutting axe from Birdbrain and cut down the stalk. The brothers quickly put the bunch, ʻahui maiʻa, in one of the mesh bags and hung it from a hau tree until they would return. Featherhead rushed onward, looking for another and different kind of banana.

Birdbrain looked at the fallen banana trunk. He knew that his grandmother liked to use strips of the black skin to weave into her lauhala mats to make a pleasant pattern. He carefully cut strips of the skin and coiled them into a roll and put them in the net with the bananas.

"Birdbrain, where are you?" called Featherhead. "Here is another! Come quickly!"

Featherhead had found a tall maiʻa haikea, the pale banana. Its fruit was thick and waxy yellow, and Featherhead knew that it could be eaten raw or cooked. The ʻahui looked perfect. Quickly he cut down the tree and the brothers put the fruit into a mesh bag and hung it from a milo tree. Featherhead rushed up the road.

After they had passed ʻOpae-leʻa village, they found a grove of wild bananas. "What about these?" Birdbrain asked.

"They are no good," Featherhead said. "The maiʻa iholena is too common. Everybody will have one. Besides, only women eat them, and we must look for a banana bunch fit for a chief."

Birdbrain saw an ʻahui maiʻa he could take back to Tūtū Nāhulu. "You are wasting your time," Featherhead said. "I won't help you carry those home."

"That's all right," Birdbrain said. "I will make another small carrying stick and carry it home on my other shoulder."

Featherhead dashed upward and out of sight. Soon Birdbrain heard a chicken crow, "Kokō! Kokō! Kokō!" and knew it was his brother crowing with delight.

He was standing beside a maiʻa ka ua lau, the many raindrops banana. The youngest hands were dark green and sprinkled with light green spots like raindrops. For a moment Birdbrain thought this bunch of bananas belonged to him but Featherhead showed him the ripe yellow-skinned fruit. Even though these were only good when cooked, Featherhead was sure that he had found a bunch of bananas worthy of the prize. Carefully he cut down the tree, placed the bunch in a bag and hung it from the branch of a kukui tree.

Birdbrain saw several pairs of eyes staring out at them from the bushes nearby. He recognized a Mū, one of the wild people who lived far up Wainiha Valley and who lived entirely on the banana. They ate raw bananas, for they did not have the secret of fire. Their clothes were made of banana leaves. Their houses were thatched with banana leaves. They planted young banana shoots in every little pocket of land up the steep sides of the cliffs as far as they could reach.

Birdbrain said to his brother, "Look, there are Mū watching us."

Featherhead said, "There are no such thing as Mū. No one has ever seen one. The Mū are only in a tale told by the storyteller. Come on, we don't have much time left before we must turn around and go home again by daylight."

Featherhead rushed up the path toward Lāʻau-haele-mai Village. Birdbrain, however, piled up a little heap of rocks and put his lunch of dried akule fish and sweet potato poi on it. "This is for you," he told the Mū, "for we are in your lands and for all I know we are taking your bananas."

As he trudged along after his brother, Birdbrain came to a tree of maiʻa puapua nui, fantail of a fowl banana. Its leaves were broad and green on the upper side and bronze on the lower side. The tall trunk was green with patches of pink and brown scattered over it. Each hand of broad-tipped fruit was perfect. There were no blemishes anywhere on the skin. Birdbrain knew that Featherhead would not want this bunch either, for it was eaten only by women and so the high chief would not want it. So Birdbrain cut down the tree and carried the ʻahui in a mesh bag back to the road and hung it from a hōlei tree to await his return.

All during that long day, the brothers searched for different kinds of bananas. They found the maiʻa koaʻe with its round yellow fruit and beautifully striped leaves, trunk, and fruit. They found a tree of maiʻa puhi, the eel banana, with its twisted fruit which was long, thick, and yellow. They found a bunch of maiʻa moa, the chicken banana, with its egg-shaped fruit growing from the tall yellowish-green trunk. They found the maiʻa ihu ʻū, the snub-nosed banana, good when cooked but bitter when raw.

Shadows filled the road as the two brothers turned toward home. As they came to each bunch of bananas in its mesh bag, they placed it carefully on the ʻauamo.

When they came to the maiʻa iholena and the maiʻa puapua nui, Featherhead refused to help. Birdbrain slung them onto a short carrying stick which he placed on his other shoulder. It was not easy to carry one long ʻauamo on one shoulder, hung with many bunches of bananas, and balance a short stick with a bunch in front and one in back, but Birdbrain thought of how pleased his grandmother would be and did not complain.

When they reached home, Birdbrain quickly hung his two bunches up where his grandmother would not see them. Then he helped Featherhead hang each of his bunches from the branches of trees. One by one, the brothers went over the fruit, pulling every dried leaf and insect from them. Each bunch must be perfect, for the chief was coming the next day. Featherhead was sure he would win the prize and fell asleep with a contented smile on his face.

After he had helped Featherhead clean his bananas, Birdbrain went to his bunches. With an old piece of tapa and a calabash of water, he cleaned each banana one by one. Only when he was satisfied he could do nothing more to improve their looks, he, too, fell asleep, with a smile of contentment.

In the morning, they heard the sound of conch shells blowing. "They're coming! They're coming!" Featherhead yelled.

"I heard," Tūtū Nāhulu said. "They are coming from the Hāʻena side."

Birdbrain said, "Tūtū Nāhulu, I have a surprise for you."

Tūtū Nāhulu replied, "A surprise? Isn't Featherhead's excitement enough?"

"No, come see," Birdbrain insisted and led his grandmother to the back of their house. He pulled off the tapa cover and looked at his grandmother's face. How he enjoyed the expression of surprise and pleasure!

"Thank you," she said and hugged Birdbrain fiercely. Then she heard the chief's conch shell and rushed back to Featherhead's side.

Featherhead stood proudly beside his many bunches of bananas. All were in wonderful condition. It would be hard to pick one as better than the others. It would depend upon what the chief preferred.

A large crowd of men and women gathered in Tūtū Nāhulu's yard. They all kneeled as the chief's retinue entered and stared at the many bunches of bananas.

Then Featherhead heard a voice say, "These are beautiful 'ahui mai'a, each one of them." Featherhead felt himself swell with pride but the voice, a woman's voice, continued, "Unfortunately, they are all forbidden for women to eat and I can't choose them."

Featherhead sat down on the ground and hung his head.

The chiefess Kilioe, who ruled the hula school at Kē'ē where the cliffs begin, sighed. "All the bananas we've seen are those permitted men. There is no point in looking any more. We shall return home."

Tūtū Nāhulu spoke up, "One more look, o Kalani, just one more look."

She beckoned and went around to the back of her house. Kilioe, curious, followed.

She saw the bunches of mai'a puapua nui and of mai'a iholena. Both could be eaten by women. "My grandson Birdbrain brought these to me," Nāhulu said.

"Why were they not in the contest, with the other bananas in the front yard?" Kilioe asked.

Tūtū Nāhulu said, "They are for a pepeie'e pudding." And she told the chiefess how the boys found their bananas.

Kilioe smiled, then she grinned, then she laughed aloud and tears came to her eyes. Then she said, "I shall take them both for they are seasoned with love. Now tell me, what can I give you in return?"

Tūtū Nāhulu replied, "The right to catch birds in all the lands under your care, after your own kia manu are through."

"All the forest birds, all the sea-going birds that nest in Hā'ena and in the mountains of Nā-pali are free to you. I only ask that you teach my kia manu your skills, for your fame goes before you. No bird, it is said, dies in the hands of your grandsons."

Then Kilioe picked two mai'a iholena. She handed one to Tūtū Nāhulu, and peeled the other for herself. "Together we will eat a banana," Kilioe said, "to mark our agreement."

After the chiefess left, Featherhead moaned, "All that work for nothing!"

Tūtū Nāhulu replied, "Invite your friends to a feast of bananas. Nothing better than to share what you have."

Birdbrain did not have time to eat any of his brother's bananas. He was too busy mixing ripe bananas and coconut cream for his grandmother's favorite pudding, pepeie'e.

Pāmāhoa

Pāmahoā stood behind her husband, Nā-koa-ola, her left arm resting on his shoulder. Yesterday Nā-koa-ola and his friends had stormed Fort Hipo at Waimea but had been driven back. During the night, the Kauaʻi forces had gathered at ʻEleʻele and formed a battle line. They watched the army of Kamehameha advancing toward them climbing the slope of ʻEleʻele toward the waiting Kauaʻi army.

Enemy drums boomed and the Kamehameha forces stopped. They lifted their rifles to their shoulders and fired. On either side of Pāmāhoa and Nā-koa-ola men fell, some crying out in agony.

Nā-koa-ola held his spear of gleaming kauila wood loosely in one hand, and from his other wrist dangled his pālau, a sharktooth-lined war club. Pāmāhoa had tucked a dagger in the waistband of her pāʻū and had armed herself with a pīkoi, a slender, crescent-shaped implement that could inflict great damage in skilled hands.

The two stood waiting, he in his mahiole, a feathered helmet, and cape, she with a lei hulu, a wreath of yellow and red feathers, wound in her hair. They were aliʻi of Kauaʻi. They were the loyal retainers of their king Kaumualiʻi. Four years ago Kaumualiʻi had been kidnapped by Liholiho and his stepmother, the evil Kaʻahumanu. He had never been allowed to return to his beloved land and those aliʻi of Kauaʻi had never been allowed to visit him. Now Kaumualiʻi was dead and the allegiance of many Kauaʻi aliʻi shifted to his son, Humehume. The land belonged to him and it should be divided amongst the chiefs of Kauaʻi in the time honored tradition stretching back to ancient times.

This had not happened. The land had been taken by Kaʻahumanu and she sent her brother to divide the land as she wished. The Kauaʻi aliʻi objected and stormed the enemy in their fort. The defenders were better armed and at dusk the Kauaʻi forces fell back to Hanapēpē.

The enemy paused. Two groups of men clustered around long round objects pulled along on their own wheels, guns bought from merchant ships that for the past forty years had sailed in and out of Hawaiian harbors. Then the guns spoke. Pāmaho'ā heard the whistle of the iron ball. It struck amongst her friends and more men fell. The Kaua'i forces shifted uneasily, not ready to retreat, knowing only death awaited them, and yet they stood in place.

"We must attack," Nā-koa-ola said. "To wait is to die." He called to his men and began to run down the hill toward the enemy, Pāmahoa running easily just behind him.

With a roar, enemy met enemy. The Kaua'i forces, armed only with wooden weapons, could not oppose the Kamehameha forces with their cannons, their rifles, their steel bayonets. Hand to hand, the Kaua'i men fought. One by one they died. Pāmāhoa saw her husband wrestling with an enemy, saw him stagger, saw the blood spurt from his throat, saw him fall. She rushed for the enemy and barely felt something fall on her head.

She awoke to the dimness of a starry night. She sat up, her head throbbing. On the plains below her there were bonfires but she knew these were not friendly to her. Around her there were the bodies of men she had known; not one stirred, there was no noise. All had died fighting for their beloved kingdom.

Beside her lay the body of Nā-koa-ola. She touched him on the shoulder but already the flesh was cold. She wanted to cry out her grief but she did not dare. She was alone on the battlefield; the enemy thought all were dead and if she cried out they would surely come and kill her.

She whispered, "Farewell, my husband." She never spoke again.

Why was she still alive? She had hoped to die beside her husband; now she alone lived. They had sworn never to leave each other; now he had gone ahead alone. Their bones would not be placed side by side so that they could wander Pō, land of the dead, together.

Her head hurt. Only one thought drove her: they would never be parted. She slung Nā-koa-ola's body over her shoulders and climbed further into the hills and down the steep narrow path into the valley of Kō'ula. Far up in the valley, she climbed partway onto the steep ridges to a cave. She made a bed of fern and laid her husband's body on it.

She never knew that in the two weeks that followed the Kamehameha forces roamed the island, killing every man, woman, and child they found that belonged to the ali'i class. Then an amnesty was declared and the dazed, frightened people began to pick up the threads of their lives again.

As days went by, then the weeks, and then months, Pāmāhoa wandered the mountains searching for 'ie'ie vines. Bit by bit she accumulated the rootlets and wove them into a basket. When only the white bones of Nā-koa-ola lay on the bed of ferns, Pāmāhoa gathered the bones and put them into the basket and wove it shut. Clasping her husband in her arms, Pāmāhoa, her eyes wild, her hair uncombed and flying free in the wind, began to wander from place to place.

The people she met were frightened of her. They knew her reason had been touched by the gods; she was sacred, so they left food for her and were glad when she wandered on, the basket clasped in her arms.

She wandered without purpose and one day, as a storm brewed in the mountains, she crossed the Wailua River and came to the dwelling place where she and her husband had stood guard over their high chief Kaumuali'i. There were pūlo'ulo'u sticks, topped with balls of white kapa, in front of it but she did not remember or care what they meant. She recalled the place and saw a large house where she had often been before. She entered the dim interior and stood quietly as though searching. Behind her, two men, soldiers fully armed, quickly entered the house and stood at Pāmāhoa's shoulders.

Seated on a hikie'e, a deep pile of lauhala mats, were two women, their attendants behind them brushing away flies with small feathered kāhili. One was twice widowed Deborah Kapule, once wife of Kaumuali'i and of Liholiho, Kamehameha's son. The other was Ka'ahumanu herself, widow of Kamehameha and of Kaumuali'i. She had come to the island to divide the land among her own family.

Irritably she looked at the wild-eyed woman. "What is she doing here?" she demanded. "Who let her in?"

One guard said, "She is Pāmāhoa. The gods have claimed her reason."

"She has broken my kapu," Ka'ahumanu replied. "Take her out and kill her." The look she gave the soldiers left no doubt of their fate if they failed their duty.

They each took Pāmāhoa by an elbow and led her outside. They marched her up the river bank until they had passed 'Ōpaeka'a Falls. They knew her story, everyone on the island knew her story, and sympathy for her overpowered the soldiers.

One said to Pāmāhoa, "Please, run away."

She stood, not understanding what was expected of her.

"Depart!" shouted the other. "Run, or we must kill you."

"Go! Do not come back while Ka'ahumanu is here."

Pāmāhoa ran. The storm broke out over her, lightning blinding her, rain pelting her skin, thunder hurting her ears, and she ran. She followed the road, crossing one river, skirting the hill of Punahunahuna, and came to the river crossing above Wai'ehu Falls. She began to cross.

She did not hear the voice of Wailua, the nymph of the river, who guarded the path across the river at the top of the falls, telling her to wait.

The river had risen and the waterfall thundered louder than Halulu, the bird of the god Kāne. The wind beat down on her, trying to tear the bundle from her arms. She waded into the river and water shoved her feet, wind tore at her, rain flowed down her arms and drenched the basket. A stronger gust knocked into Pāmāhoa, her feet slipped, and instinctively she flung out her arms to keep her balance.

The basket flew out over the edge of the waterfall and fell into the raging pool below.

Pāmāhoa screamed, a long wild bitter cry of agony that chilled the nymph Wailua.

Pāmāhoa stood at the top of the falls, staring down. Then she saw the face of her husband, in the water. Nā-koa-ola smiled at her. "Come!" he called, "Come!"

Pāmāhoa stepped to the edge and jumped.

He 'ike mo'olelo na ke kuhi wale. A tale, this, wrung from my heart.

The Sources of the Tales

From time to time I am asked where I find the tales of Kaua'i that I retell.

Each story has several different sources, most of them in now out-of-print books, in papers stuffed in files in some library or archive, or in Hawaiian newspapers only available on microfilm. Some are tales I remember being told as a youngster by master storytellers. Over the past twenty or so years, I have gathered all references to any Kaua'i legend or tale I came across, even a brief line in a chant. In time, a story comes to light. Sometimes only tantalizing tidbits hint at a lost story. The sources are varied and sometimes unusual.

For instance, in an obscure bibliography I saw a reference to a contest held at Kamehameha School for Girls in 1938. I contacted Sigrid Southworth, head librarian of Kamehameha Schools. She had never heard of it but searched her files and found the actual papers written for submission. Martha Beckwith, the noted anthropologist, had offered a prize for the best legend submitted. Each girl was asked to go home, ask an elder for a legend, and write it down. From this source came several legends found nowhere else.

More specifically, here are the particular sources of the stories within this book.

'Alekoko

Ellis, Harriet. "The Legend of the Niumalu Fishpond." Ms. submitted for the Martha Beckwith Prize, 1942. Kamehameha School Library, Honolulu.

Hofgaard, C.B. "Who were the Menehunes?" *Paradise of the Pacific,* May 1, 1928: 9.

Rice, Charles A. Personal interview. 1930s.

Hanakā'ape

Pukui, Mary Kawena, trans. "A Hawaiian Legend of a Terrible War between Pele-of-the-Eternal-Fires and Waka-of-the-Shadowy-Waters." *Ka Loea Kalaiaina,* May 13 - Dec. 20, 1899.

He Ka'ao no ka 'Ōhelo Kahi

Gay, Francis. *Place Names of Kaua'i.* Ts. Kauai Historical Society, Lihue.

He Ka'ao o Kakala a me 'A'awa

Ferreira, Juliet. "The Story of the Caterpillar." Ms. submitted for the Martha Beckwith Prize, 1938. Kamehemeha Schools Library, Honolulu.

Hiku a me Kāwelu

Beckwith, Martha Warren. *Hawaiian Mythology.* Honolulu: University of Hawaii Press, 1919.

Knudsen, Eric A. *Teller of Hawaiian Tales.* Honolulu: Mutual Publishing, 1946.

Fornander, Abraham. "Fornander Collection of Hawaiian Antiquities and Folklore." *Memoirs of the Bernice Pauahi Bishop Museum,* 5 (1917, 1918): 182.

Thrum, Thomas G. *Hawaiian Folktales.* Chicago: A.C. McClurg and Co., 1907.

Westervelt, W.D., trans. *Hawaiian Legends of Ghosts and Ghost-gods.* Rutland, Vt.: Charles E. Tuttle, 1964. (First ed. published in 1915 under the title *Legents of Gods and Ghosts.*)

Kahalahala

Dickey, Lyle A. "String Figures from Hawaii, Including Some from New Hebrides and Gilbert Islands." *Bernice P. Bishop Museum Bulletin,* 54 (1928): 169.

Knudsen, Eric A. *Teller of Hawaiian Tales.* Honolulu: Mutual Publishing, 1946.

Pukui, Mary Kawena, trans. *'Ōlelo No'eau, Hawaiian Proverbs and Poetical Sayings.* Honolulu: Bernice P. Bishop Museum Special Publication No. 71, 1983.

Ka Ho'okolokolo o 'Elepaio

Thrum, Thomas G. "Story of the Elepaio." *Paradise of the Pacific,* Dec. 1, 1925: 70.

Dickey, Lyle A. "String Figures from Hawaii, Including Some from New Hebrides and Gilbert Islands." *Bernice P. Bishop Museum Bulletin,* 54 (1928): 169.

Ka Moena Hohola o Mānā

Hadley, Thelma H. and Margaret S. Williams. *Kauai, the Garden Island of Hawaii.* Lihue: Garden Island Publishing Company, 1962.

Ka-wai-o-Maliu

Akina, J.A. *The Story of the Menehune People, as Selected and Arranged as Told from the Memories of the Old Men of Waimea as far as Mana,* transcribed by Frances Frazier. Ms.

Rice, William Hyde. *Hawaiian Legends.* Honolulu: Bishop Museum Press, 1977.

Ka-wai-o-Palai

Dole, C.S. "National Park for Garden Island." *Paradise of the Pacific,* Dec. 1, 1916: 50.

Lydgate, J.M. "Charm and Romance of Haena, Kauai." *Paradise of the Pacific,* Dec. 1, 1922: 146.

Ke Kahua o Maliʻo

Hadley, Thelma H. and Margaret S. Williams. *Kauai, the Garden Island of Hawaii.* Lihue: Garden Island Publishing Company, 1962.

Māmā-akua-Lono

Lahainaluna Student Compositions. Hms. Misc 43, No. 19, Bernice P. Bishop Museum Archives, Honolulu.

Nā Kia Manu a me Nā Maiʻa

Gay, Francis. *Place Names of Kauaʻi.* Ts. Kauai Historical Society, Lihue.

Kekahuna, Henry. Notes. Kekahuna Collection, Hawaii Archives, Honolulu.

Nā Kia Manu a me Nā Moa Makanahele

Gay, Francis. *Place Names of Kauaʻi.* Ts. Kauai Historical Society, Lihue.

Mea Kakau. "He wahi moolelo Hawaii." *Nupepa Kuokoa,* June 27, 1902: 4.

Rice, William Hyde. *Hawaiian Legends.* Honolulu: Bishop Museum Press, 1977.

Pāmāhoa

Emerson, Nathaniel B. *Unwritten Literature of Hawaii: The Sacred Songs of the Hula, Collected and Translated with Notes and an Account of the Hula.* Rutland, Vt.: Charles E. Tuttle, 1915. Rpt. of *Bureau of American Ethnology Bulletin 38,* 1909.

Pīkoi a me Puapualenalena

Fornander, Abraham. "Fornander Collection of Hawaiian Antiquities and Folklore." *Memoirs of the Bernice Pauahi Bishop Museum,* 5 (1917, 1918): 182.

'Ualaka'a

Kekahuna, Henry. "The Story of Ualakaa." Ms. Kekahuna Collection, Hawaii Archives, Honolulu.

Fornander, Abraham. "Fornander Collection of Hawaiian Antiquities and Folklore." *Memoirs of the Bernice Pauahi Bishop Museum,* 5 (1917, 1918): 182.

Weoweo-pilau

Hadley, Thelma H. and Margaret S. Williams. *Kauai, the Garden Island of Hawaii.* Lihue: Garden Island Publishing Company, 1962.

Rice, Charles A. Personal interview. 1930s.

About the Author

Frederick B. Wichman is the author of *Kaua'i Tales* and *Polihale and Other Kaua'i Legends*. He often gives lectures and readings concerning the stories and place names of his home island. He lives at Ha'ena, a land rich with legends.

About the Illustrator

The sun drenched landscape of Kaua'i is where kama-'aina artist Christine Fayé makes her home. In 1993, she received the Hawai'i Book Publishers Association Ka Palapala Po'okela Award for her illustrations in Frederick B. Wichman's *Kaua'i Tales*.